The Contented Baby's First Year

The Contented Baby's First Year

The secret to a calm and
contented baby

Gina Ford

Vermilion

PHOTOGRAPHY BY SANDRA LOUSADA

7 9 10 8 6

Published in 2007 by Vermilion, an imprint of Ebury Publishing

Ebury Publishing is a division of the Random House Group

The Random House Group Limited Reg. No. 954009

Addresses for companies within the Random House Group
can be found at
www.randomhouse.co.uk

A CIP catalogue record for this book is available
from the British Library

The Random House Group Limited supports The Forest Stewardship
Council (FSC), the leading international forest certification organisation. All our
titles that are printed on Greenpeace approved FSC certified paper carry the FSC logo.
Our paper procurement policy can be found at
www.rbooks.co.uk/environment

Printed and bound by Firmengruppe APPL, aprinta druck,Wemding, Germany

ISBN 9780091912741

Please note that conversions to imperial weights and measures are
suitable equivalents and not exact.

The information given in this book should not be treated as a substitute
for qualified medical advice; always consult a medical practitioner.
Neither the author nor the publisher can be held responsible for any loss
or claim arising out of the use, or misuse, of the suggestions made or the
failure to take medical advice.

Contents

Introduction 6
Welcoming Your Baby to the World 8

The
First
Month 30

The
Second
Month 66

The
Third
Month 84

The
Fourth
Month 98

The
Fifth
Month 114

The
Sixth
Month 132

The
Seventh
Month 152

The
Eighth
Month 168

The
Ninth
Month 182

The
Tenth
Month 196

The
Eleventh
Month 210

The
Twelfth
Month 220

Useful addresses and Further reading 234
Index 236
About the Author 240
Acknowledgements 240

Introduction

My first book, *The Contented Little Baby Book*, famous for its feeding and sleeping routines, became a bestseller through word of mouth recommendation. In *The Contented Baby's First Year*, I am delighted to have the opportunity to introduce another dimension to the Contented Little Baby phenomenon. With photographs of beautiful babies, I have been able to illustrate some of my personal methods, bringing the Contented Little Baby routines 'to life'. It has been a joy for me to produce *The Contented Baby's First Year*, and I hope that it compliments my original book while contributing something new and special to baby care.

As parents of a newborn baby, you have a wonderful new world opening up before you. It can be a daunting prospect, and I very much hope that this book will guide, encourage and support you during that extraordinary first year. The role of a parent comes with an entirely new set of challenges, but above all it is an immensely rewarding and emotionally enriching experience.

You may feel a little anxious, faced with the precious new life you have created. Your baby is utterly dependant on you and it is a huge and humbling responsibility to have to care for him so completely. *The Contented Baby's First Year* demonstrates how to settle, feed, comfort and interact with your new baby.

In the early days with your baby, feeding, changing and dressing your newborn can seem all-consuming, but very soon your baby's daily care will become second nature and you will have more time to enjoy and respond to his individual needs. You may be surprised at the constant change and development your baby undergoes during his first year, as he acquires the basic skills he needs for the future – sitting, crawling, eating, playing, walking and talking, to name but a few. With *The Contented Baby's First Year*, you can follow your baby's development month by month, and will be empowered to understand, enjoy and encourage his personal, mental and physical progress. Do remember, however, that all babies are individuals and develop at different rates, so don't worry if your baby is not at exactly the same stage as those of your friends.

The huge number of requests from parents for a more in-depth and detailed guide to childcare and development has inspired me to write this book. I hope that the information and the beautiful photographs will prove helpful and encouraging, assisting your newly-acquired knowledge as parents, and that the Contented Little Baby routines, which have worked for many thousands of parents, will work for you too.

And finally, you'll notice that throughout the book the baby is referred to as 'he'. This is purely for consistency and clarity and 'he' could just as easily have been 'she'.

GINA

Welcoming your baby to the world

AFTER MANY MONTHS OF WAITING, THE FIRST TIME THAT YOU SEE your baby is certain to be one of the most exciting and memorable moments of your life. Nothing can quite prepare you for the sight of your newborn's tiny face gazing back at yours. At the same time it will probably strike you that life is never going to be the same again – this little person is now dependant on you for everything. As a new parent there will be much to learn in the months ahead but getting to know your baby and his individual needs and tastes is sure to be the most challenging and rewarding experience. The first twelve months of your baby's life are a time of extremely rapid growth and development, when you will see the most fascinating changes occur from one month to the next. Your one-year-old child will be very different, both physically and mentally, to the tiny newborn that is snuggled up to you now.

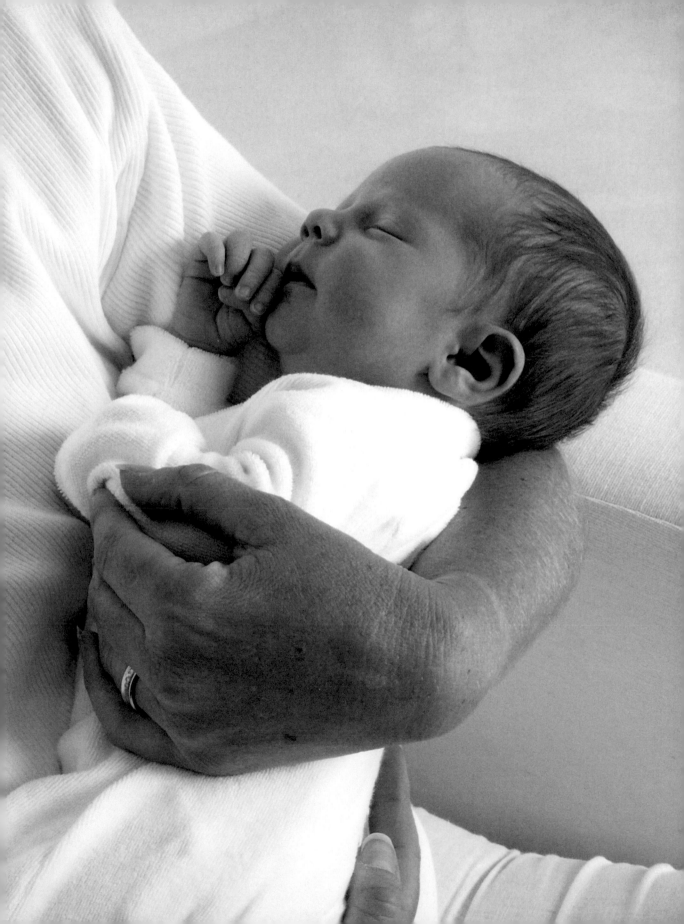

Your newborn baby

Newborn babies all have their own individual characteristics but there are certain features that many newborns have in common.

Toes and fingers

Newborns' fingers and toes are very flexible and they have a natural grasping reflex, which you will notice if you place your finger into your baby's palm. Your baby's nails are very soft although they will soon become sharp enough for him to scratch himself. You will need to trim the nails regularly with special baby nail scissors when they become overlong. The best time to do this is after your baby has had his bath and has been fed and is sleepy. The nails are softer after they've been in the water. Scratch mittens can also be bought for young babies to wear.

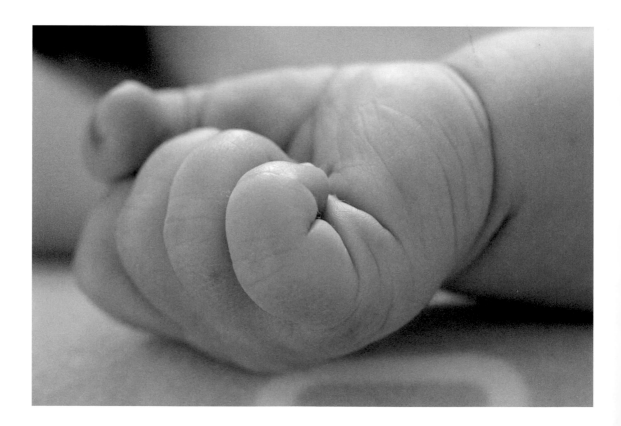

The head

Not all newborns' heads are perfectly shaped. Your baby's head may appear quite narrow and long due to the pressure of having been squeezed through the birth canal. It will gradually recover and become more of a rounded shape in time. There may also be red marks, bruising or slight swelling on the head, particularly if you have had a forceps delivery. Your baby's eyes may also be a little red and puffy and his nose slightly flattened. This is all completely normal and your baby's features will soon recover from the delivery.

The fontanelles

If you look closely at the top of your baby's head you will see a small soft area that is moving slightly, or 'pulsing'. This is a fontanelle, a spot where the bones of the skull have not yet fused together, allowing room for the baby's brain to grow. There are two fontanelles: one is found at the top and front of the head, the other is located towards the back of the head and is harder to find. Both fontanelles are protected by tough membranes and will eventually close up.

Your baby's head may appear quite narrow and long due to the pressure of having been squeezed through the birth canal

Birthmarks

Birthmarks come in a huge range of shapes and sizes and many babies have at least one birthmark somewhere on their body. Some birthmarks disappear eventually, others are permanent.

Hair

Babies differ hugely when it comes to hair – some are born completely bald, others emerge with a generous head of hair. This early hair usually falls out in the first month and may be of a completely different colour to the hair your baby will grow later. Some babies, particularly premature ones, have a fine downy layer of hair growing on their back and shoulders. This should fall off naturally in the first few weeks.

Skin

While your baby has been growing inside you, his skin has been protected with a waxy coating called vernix. This comes off soon after birth but your baby's skin may peel for a while. Your baby may also have blotchy skin or tiny whitish bumps on the surface of his skin. These are blocked pores that will disappear in a few weeks' time when the baby's pores begin to open. If you choose to use a cream or lotion, make sure you look for ones that are baby-friendly.

Umbilical cord

Your newborn will have a strange-looking brown stump on his tummy, which is the remainder of the cut umbilical cord. The stump has no nerves so it is not at all painful for the baby. It should drop off by itself within two weeks to reveal a healthy belly button but in the meantime it is best left alone, apart from gentle cleansing with cotton wool and cooled boiled water. If you're unsure how to do this ask your midwife or health visitor and if you get any sense that it may be infected, seek medical attention.

Breathing

Some newborn babies can be very snuffly breathers and many new parents are unduly alarmed by some of the noises their babies make. Newborns do not always appear to be breathing regularly and they may take irregular short and long breaths in the first few weeks, before they settle down to a pattern of more regular breathing.

The first 24 hours

All births are different. You may be feeling sore and exhausted after giving birth, as well as feeling all kinds of emotions following the upheaval of labour. The effect of all the hormones surging through your body may make you feel tearful and upset or, conversely, elated and on a post-childbirth 'high'. However the experience affects you personally, it is natural for many

Don't be afraid to ask for help if you need it – friends and family can be of enormous support, and even a neighbour can help out with the shopping

first-time parents to feel unsure about their ability to look after their newborn, who seems so delicate and fragile. If you have given birth in a hospital, taking your baby home for the first time may feel nerve-racking, but you will soon get used to looking after your baby in his new surroundings. The first few weeks are incredibly exhausting so don't be afraid to ask for help if you need it – friends and family can be of enormous support and even a neighbour can help out with the shopping.

The first feed

As a new parent, you will be probably be wondering how often and for how long you should be feeding your baby. Whether your baby is breastfed or bottle-fed, it takes time to establish a proper feeding routine so do not worry if things do not immediately fall into place. Straight after the birth you will be encouraged by the midwife to put your baby to the breast to suckle. Your milk will not yet be in but you will be producing an important fluid called colostrum, which is higher in protein and vitamins than the mature milk that is produced later. Colostrum also contains antibodies that will help your baby resist any infections that you have had.

- Newborns need to feed little and often, as their tummies are very tiny.

- During the early days most babies will probably need to feed between eight and 12 times a day and some even more than this.

- Do not be tempted to restrict feeds at this time, as feeding little and often is one of the best ways of ensuring that you establish a good milk supply. However, it will not help you produce more milk if your baby is not latched on to the breast properly.

- Poor positioning is the most common cause of cracked and painful nipples, which is one of the main reasons many mothers give up breastfeeding within a matter of weeks.

- When you are in hospital you should be given advice by your midwife regarding the positioning of your baby on the breast. However, because your stay in hospital is likely to be no longer than 48 hours, I would urge that you seek the advice of an experienced breastfeeding counsellor who can visit you once you are at home.

- While the advice I give will help you grasp the basics of breastfeeding, it is no substitute for personal one-to-one guidance.

- Arranging a home visit from a breastfeeding counsellor the first day you are out of hospital, followed up by a second visit within a day or so, will help get you off to the best possible start with breastfeeding.

Starting off a routine

Some newborns are very sleepy and, if this is the case with your baby, I recommend waking him and offering five minutes on each breast every three hours, gradually increasing the feeding time until your milk comes in. This should happen somewhere between the third and the fifth day, by which time your baby should be feeding for about 15-20 minutes at a time. Your aim is to settle your baby into a three-hourly feeding routine (this is calculated from the beginning of one feed to the beginning of the next). Many babies will now be getting enough milk from the first breast and will be happy to go three hours till the next feed. Not all babies need the second breast in the early days. If your baby has emptied the first breast, burp him, change his nappy, then offer him the second breast. If he needs more he will take it, if not, start him on the second breast at the next feed. If you find your baby is hungry before the three hours have passed, he should, of course, be fed. If your baby is feeding much longer than the suggested time and is hungry again an hour or so later, you should seek advice from a breastfeeding counsellor.

Breastfeeding tips

- When your milk first comes in your baby may find it difficult to 'latch on' to the engorged breast. Expressing a little milk before feeding will help. This can be done by placing warm wet flannels on the breast and gently squeezing milk from the nipples.

- It is important that your baby empties the first breast before he starts the second. If you change breasts too soon, your baby may be getting too much fore milk, which I believe is one of the causes of babies suffering from colic. The richer hind milk comes after the fore milk and it may take a sleepy baby as long as 25 minutes to reach it.

- Waking your baby to feed every three hours in the early days allows your nipples to get used to his sucking and stimulates your milk production. It will also help ease the pain of engorgement when the milk arrives.

- If you're planning to follow a routine, expressing extra milk in the early days will help establish a good milk supply.

- If you aim to feed your baby three-hourly between 6am and midnight, you will be getting a feeding routine off to the best possible start. Even a very young baby is capable of going one longer spell in between feeds. Following this advice should ensure that this happens at night rather than in the daytime, thus avoiding the 'feeding all night' syndrome. For more detailed information on breast and formula-feeding, see page 32.

Limiting visitors

The arrival of a new baby in a family is always a time for joy and much excitement, and you will, of course, want to share this special time with grandparents and close family and friends. However, it is important to try and allow enough time for you and your partner to get to know your baby and to learn how to handle him and to deal with his many needs confidently. This can often be difficult if you have a continuous flow of visitors interrupting feeding and bathing times, and giving their opinions on how things should be done.

'BABYMOON'
The first weeks are often called 'the babymoon' and this should be a special time for you to get to know and to be close to your baby. Remember, this is your baby so do not feel selfish about having your 'babymoon' as this time will never come again. There will be lots of opportunities for family and friends to get more involved in the months ahead.

I know from personal experience that parents who made sure that they had enough quiet time with their baby in the early days learned how to deal confidently with the day-to-day care much more quickly than those who constantly surrounded themselves with visitors.

Babies are very receptive to voices, touch and body language. Even as a newborn, a baby is acutely sensitive to how his needs are handled. In the early days, when he is getting used to the world around him, it is better if most of his needs are met by the two most important people in his life – his parents. If you are able to handle your baby calmly and with confidence, he will respond by being a calm and contented baby.

Babies thrive on plenty of close physical contact. Cuddling and comforting your baby play a huge part in helping the bonding process, but you should bear in mind that he will get tired very quickly. All too often I have witnessed a sleeping baby being handed from one visitor to the next, only to scream for hours long after the visitors had left. This results in the parents becoming distressed and anxious as they think that they are not responding to their baby's needs properly. The reality is that the baby has become physically and mentally exhausted by all the handling. At the point when the parents have to deal with feeding and changing, the baby is, of course, overtired and fractious as a result of all the overstimulation.

Holding and handling your newborn baby

In the early days after the birth you will spend most of the time that your baby is awake holding and handling him. How you handle him during feeding, burping, changing, bathing, dressing and settling him to sleep will have a big impact on how he responds to the new world he has just entered.

The following suggestions explain how to pick your baby up and put him down properly so that he feels safe and secure. It is important to remember that a newborn baby's head and neck must always be supported as his muscles are not yet strong enough for him to hold his own head up. Whatever position you choose, one hand should always be supporting your baby's head.

Babies thrive on plenty of close physical contact; cuddling and comforting your baby play a huge part in helping the bonding process

Picking your baby up

- Make sure you are close enough to pick your baby up comfortably. Bend over and, as you start to pick him up, tell him what you are doing. I found that saying, 'Up you come' to babies each time I picked them up helped them to understand what was going to happen; within weeks you could feel them stiffen their neck muscles in preparation for being picked up.

- Slide one hand under his head and neck, spreading your fingers out to support his head, then slide the other hand between his legs.

- As you lift your baby closer to you, straighten your back, and gently move the hand that is supporting his head further down his back until his head is in the crook of your arm.

- Once his head is in the crook of your arm, you can then move your supporting arm around so that his bottom is resting on your forearm, and you can use your hand to hold the bottom of his legs close to your body. This holding position will keep your baby from thrashing his legs around and make him feel more secure.

Putting your baby down

- As you lower your baby down, bring the hand that you are supporting your baby with further up his back, until it is supporting his neck. At the same time use your other hand to hold and support his bottom.

- Remember to tell him what you are doing, saying, 'Down you go' as you are lowering him.

- Once he is lying flat, slide your hand out from under his bottom, and then gently slide the other one from under his head.

Holding your baby

This is the most commonly used holding position, but it is a good idea to get used to adopting different ways of holding your baby. The descriptions below and opposite show four other positions that I use, depending on the baby's needs at the time.

Across your chest

Holding the baby across your chest when he is fretful or overtired is a great way to get him to calm down.

Over the shoulder

This position can be used to burp the baby, or to walk him around the room when he is getting bored or fractious.

His back to your tummy

This is a great way to hold him when he is bored as it allows you to hold him closely, but also facing outwards so that he can look at different objects, pictures, etc. as you walk around the room.

Face down on the crook of your arm

This is another position that is really good if the baby is fractious or bothered by wind.

Nappy changing

During the first month you will find that you are changing your baby's nappy anywhere between eight and 12 times a day. By changing your baby's nappy every time he has a bowel movement, and before the nappy gets really wet, you are reducing the risk of your baby's bottom becoming red and irritated. You are also avoiding the likelihood of nappy rash, which can be incredibly painful.

While it is important to change your baby's nappy frequently, do not become obsessive about it. For example, if your baby wakes up and is yelling for a feed, as long as he doesn't have a very wet or dirty nappy, it makes sense to allow him enough of a feed to calm him down before changing him.

Most babies move their bowels during the middle of a feed anyway, so changing the nappy at the beginning of the feed may mean that your

SKIN IRRITATION
Some babies are more vulnerable to skin irritation and nappy rash than others. Allowing your baby to kick for short spells during the day without his nappy on allows the air to reach his skin and will help keep it healthy and rash-free.

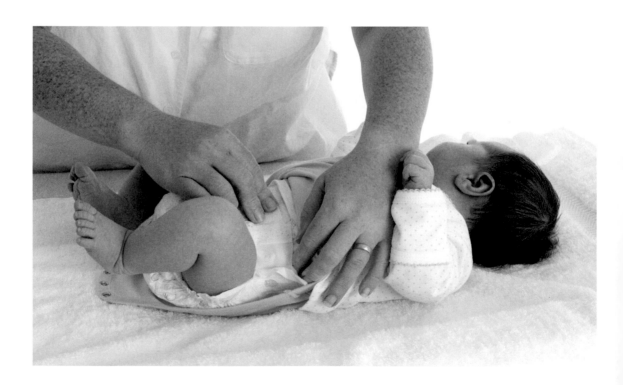

baby is only in the clean nappy for 10 or 15 minutes before it needs to be changed again. Changing the nappy midway through a feed is also a great way of rousing a baby, who keeps falling asleep while feeding.

You should also ensure that you check and, if necessary, change your baby's nappy before you settle him down for a sleep. In the middle of the night, only change the baby's nappy if it is dirty or very wet. However, if your baby has very sensitive skin, then it may be advisable to change his nappy even if it is only slightly wet, rather than risk his skin becoming red and irritated.

Lots of newborn babies hate having their nappy changed, so the speedier you can make it, the better. Check regularly that you have all the supplies you need to hand by his changing table.

In the early days I always recommend that baby wipes are avoided. Warm water and cotton wool are all that is really needed. When out and about, if using baby wipes, try to choose ones that are perfume-free and formulated for sensitive skin. Avoid using baby powder, as it clogs the skin and can get into the lungs.

TOP TIP
If you live in a house with lots of stairs it is worth considering a second changing mat and small plastic bowl for downstairs, so that you are not running up and down the stairs every time your baby needs a nappy change.

How to change a nappy

You will need: nappy, cotton wool pads, soft tissues, bowl of cooled boiled water, barrier cream for bottom

There are a variety of disposable and reusable nappies available nowadays. Disposable nappies have adjustable Velcro tabs at the top while reusable nappies come in various styles: traditional terry towelling squares which are pinned or clipped into place or preshaped nappies which are fastened with poppers, Velcro or an outer wrap. You will usually need to use a disposable nappy liner inside the reusable nappy with a pair of waterproof pants on the outside.

During the first month you will find that you are changing your baby's nappy anywhere between 8 and 12 times a day

- Lay your baby on his back on a changing mat on a safe firm surface. Lift his babygrow or vest right up and away from his bottom to avoid it getting dirty in case there are leakages while you are changing the nappy.

- If using a disposable, open the nappy and roll it up towards your baby to contain any stools that may be there. With a reusable, remove the nappy liner and dispose of it according to the manufacturer's instructions.

- Take your baby's ankles in one hand, gently pushing his legs backwards so that his bottom is lifted slightly. Using some soft tissue, wipe the remainder of any stools from your baby's bottom. Gently slide the nappy out and put it to one side for disposal in a nappy bag or place in a bucket for washing.

- Open your baby's legs wide apart, and with a damp cotton wool pad, wipe all around your baby's tummy area and the creases of the legs.

- Wash from front to back using a clean damp cotton wool pad. Front-to-back washing is particularly important for the prevention of urinary infections in girls. With boys, it is a good idea to put a small cloth over the penis when changing to avoid urine squirting into his (or your) face. Hold the penis down when the clean nappy is put on to prevent urine leaking out of the top.

- Dry your baby's bottom and creases well with a fresh cotton pad or tissue.

- Take your baby's ankles in one hand again, raising his bottom as you do so, and then slip the clean opened nappy under his bottom. With cloth nappies the widest part should go under your baby's waist. If using a disposable, the side with the tapes attached should be underneath the baby and level with his waist.

Wash your baby from front to back to prevent him getting a urinary infection

- Using one finger, take a small amount of barrier cream and spread it around your baby's bottom and in the creases. Remember to wipe your finger with a tissue before touching the nappy again as the cream will stop the tapes sticking.

- Bring your baby's legs down, and then push the front of the nappy up across his tummy towards his waist.

- Finally, unpeel the tapes and stick them down or use pins, clips or poppers to fasten the nappy, making sure that it fits securely, but not too tightly.

- Place your baby in his cot, or in a safe place, while you wash your hands.

THE FIRST NAPPY

Most babies have their first bowel movement within 48 hours of birth. The nappy will be filled with a sticky, black-green substance called meconium, which has been stored inside the baby's intestines before birth. Later nappies will vary in colour: the stools of a breastfed baby are usually yellowish and mustard-like in consistency, while a bottle-fed baby's stools are thicker and darker. Your newborn should urinate frequently so his nappies will need frequent changing. For more on nappy changing, see page 21.

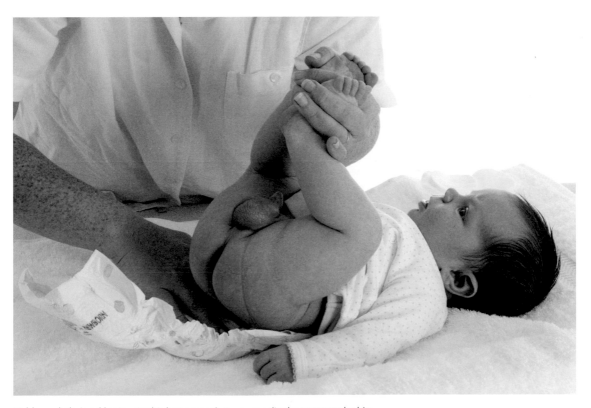

Hold your baby's ankles to raise his bottom so that you can slip the nappy under him

Nappy rash

Nappy rash can make a baby very unsettled and can be very painful, particularly if the irritated skin comes into contact with urine or stools. If your baby does get nappy rash, ensure that you change his nappies even more frequently and give him time to kick with his nappy off so that air can circulate around the skin. If you use reusable nappies, replace with disposables at nap and bedtimes until the rash clears up. Using cotton wool, clean the area with unscented baby oil, and apply a thin layer of good-quality barrier cream. If the rash hasn't cleared up within a few days, then your baby should be seen by a doctor as it may be a candida rash (often referred to as thrush) and will need a special anti-fungal cream.

Crying

I have read research which claims that most young babies cry on average for a total of two hours in a day. With very young babies I have noticed that they do go through a more unsettled stage around three weeks and six weeks of age, which tends to coincide with growth spurts. However, I would be absolutely horrified if any of the babies I have looked after cried for even one hour a day, let alone two! The one thing my parents comment on, time and time again, is how happy their babies are when following my guidelines. Of course all babies cry, some when they are having their nappy changed, others when having their faces washed and a few try to fight sleep when they are put in their cots. With the ones that fight sleep, because I know that they are well fed, burped and ready to sleep, I let them fuss and cry for five to 10 minutes until they settle themselves. This is the only real crying I experience and even then it is with the minority of babies and lasts for no longer than a

When your baby is tiny and fretful, it is wise to assume that when he cries the problem is hunger and you should offer him a feed

week or two. Understandably, all parents hate to hear their baby cry and many are worried that to let their baby cry for a short while prior to sleeping could be psychologically damaging. I would like to reassure you that, provided your baby has been well fed and that you have followed the advice regarding awake periods and wind-down time, your baby will not suffer psychological damage. In the long term you will have a happy, contented baby who has learned to settle himself to sleep.

Listed below are the main reasons a healthy baby would cry. Use it as a checklist to eliminate the possible cause for your baby crying. At the top of the list is hunger. A tiny baby who is hungry should always be fed if necessary.

Possible reasons for crying

Hunger

When your baby is very tiny and fretful, it is wise to assume that when he cries the problem is hunger and to offer him a feed even if it is well before the time I recommend for his age. One of the main reasons that I find very young breastfed babies are unsettled in the evening is usually hunger. If your baby feeds well, stays awake for a short spell after feeds, then sleeps well until the next feed, but is unsettled in the evening, it is very possible that the cause is hunger. Many mothers can produce a lot of milk early on in the day, but come the evening, when tiredness has crept in, the milk supply can decrease dramatically. I would strongly recommend that for a few nights you try topping your baby up with a small amount of expressed milk after his bath. If he settles well you will know your milk supply is low in the evening.

Tiredness

Babies under six weeks tend to get tired after one hour of being awake. Although they may not be quite ready to sleep they need to be kept quiet and calm. Not all babies show obvious signs of tiredness, so, in the early days, after they have been awake for one hour, I would advise that you take them to their room or a peaceful part of the house to wind down gradually.

Overtiredness

No baby under three months should be allowed to stay awake for more than two hours at a time, as they can become very overtired and difficult to settle.

An overtired or overstimulated baby may reach a stage where he is unable to drift off to sleep naturally, and the more tired he becomes, the more he fights sleep. A baby under three months who is allowed to get into this state can become almost impossible to settle. In a situation like this, sometimes a short period of 'crying down' has to be used as a last resort to solve the problem. This is the only situation where I would advise that very young babies are left to cry for a short period, and even then it can only be done if you are confident that the baby has been well fed and winded.

Boredom

Even a newborn baby needs to be awake and stimulated some of the time. Encourage him to be awake for a short spell after his day feeds and use bright, noisy toys for social times and calm, soothing ones for sleepy times. Babies under one month love to look at anything black and white, especially pictures of faces. Of course, the faces that will fascinate them the most will be the ones of their mummy and daddy.

Wind

All babies take in a certain amount of wind when they are feeding. Given the opportunity, most babies bring up their wind easily (see page 42 for advice). If you think that wind is the cause of your baby's crying, check that you are allowing enough time between feeds.

A breastfed baby needs at least three hours to digest a full feed, while a formula-fed baby should be allowed three to four hours. This time is calculated from the beginning of one feed to the beginning of the next.

I would also suggest that you keep an eye on your baby's weight gain. If it is in excess of 240–300g (8–10oz) a week and he appears to be suffering from wind pains, it could be that he is overfeeding. See page 39 for advice on how to deal with this.

Colic

Colic is a common problem for babies under three months and it can make life miserable for both the baby and his parents. Parents describe how their baby screams, often for hours at a time, thrashes madly and brings his legs up in pain. The most common time for this seems to be between 6pm and midnight. Colic usually disappears by four months of age but by then the baby has learnt all the wrong sleep associations as the parents have had to resort to endless rocking, patting and driving around the block, most of which seems to bring little or no relief.

In my experience, 'colicky' babies seem to have one thing in common; they

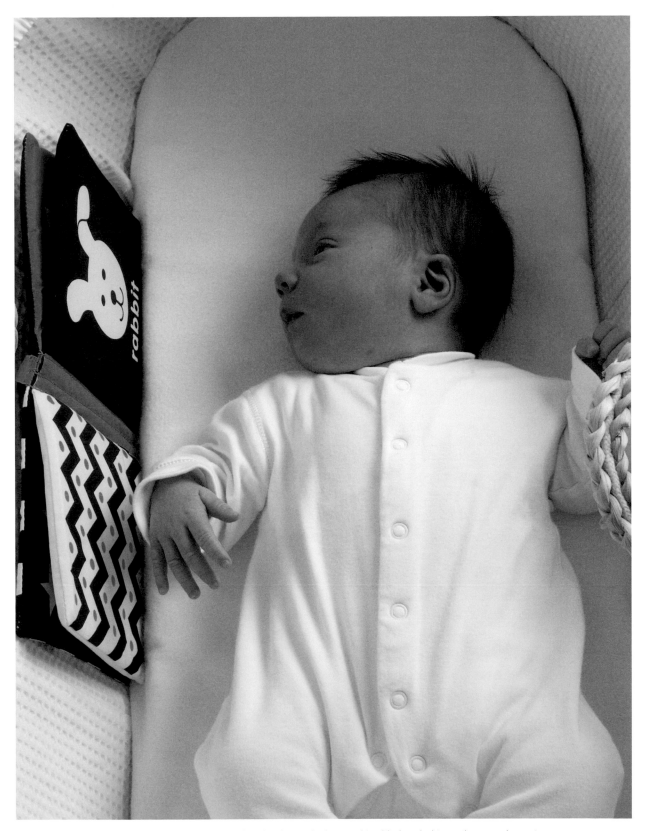

Newborn babies need stimulation when they are awake; they love to look at anything black and white as these are the easiest shades on which they can focus

are all being fed on demand. Feeding this way all too often leads to the baby having a feed before the previous one has been digested, one of the reasons that I believe may be the cause of colic.

The babies I cared for never suffered from colic and I am convinced this is because their feeding and sleeping has been structured from day one. When I was called to help older babies who were suffering from colic it seemed to disappear very quickly once I structured their feeding and sleeping. With older babies who were often feeding every two hours night and day, and gaining excessive amounts of weight each week, I found that by replacing one of the night feeds with some sugar water – 120ml (4oz) of cooled boiled water mixed with half a teaspoon of sugar – to settle them, they would immediately go a longer spell of nearer three hours, which meant they fed more and then settled to sleep again for a further longer spell.

In the morning I would always wake the baby at 7am, regardless of how little sleep he had had in the night, and then proceed with a regular feeding and sleeping schedule for his age until 6.30pm in the evening. At this time I would always offer all breastfed babies a top-up of expressed milk to ensure that they had had enough to eat, and would settle well in the evening. If the baby was unsettled after the feed I would use the method described on page 48 to settle him. This would help avoid him having to feed again in two hours, which is a common pattern of colicky babies. With a bottle-fed baby I always make sure that the 2.30pm feed is smaller so that he feeds well at 6.30pm. With a baby of three months or more I would attempt to eliminate middle-of-the-night feeds altogether, or at least reduce feeds to only one. Once the baby's feeding and sleeping pattern became more regular during the day and a pattern of once-a-night waking was established I would gradually reduce the amount of sugar in the sugar-water solution until he was taking plain water. While many breastfed babies may continue to need one middle-of-the-night feed until they are weaned at six months, provided they are having full feeds between 6/7am and 10/11pm they should not need to feed several times a night, which is a common problem in colicky babies.

Parents are often concerned that sugar water will rot their baby's teeth. Because of the short time that it is used, I have never encountered this

> A common time for babies to suffer from colic seems to be between 6pm and midnight

problem. My advice has been backed up by research by Dr Peter Lewindon of the Royal Children's Hospital, Brisbane, Australia, which has shown that sugar stimulates the body's natural painkillers and that some babies can be helped by sugar-water solution.

Colic usually disappears by four months of age but by then the baby has learnt all the wrong sleep associations as the parents have had to resort to endless rocking, patting and driving around the block.

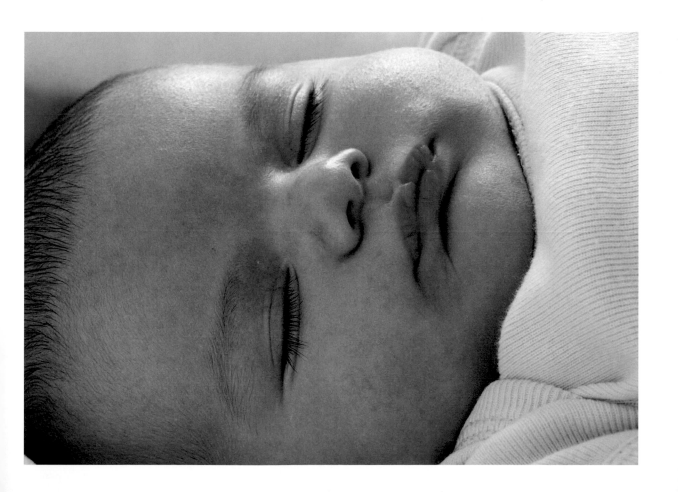

The
First
Month

THE FIRST MONTH WITH YOUR NEWBORN BABY IS A PARTICULARLY special time, and one to be treasured. Do try to focus on the moment and use this 'babymoon period' to get to know this unique new life you have created. Make sure you have lots of time on your own as parents to get to know your baby; to make him feel loved and secure, comfortable and warm. The more you are able to understand your baby's needs, the calmer and more confident you will become as parents, and the more contented your baby will be.

In the early days, breastfeeding every couple of hours can be exhaustin and all too often the excitement of a new baby can attract such a constant stream of visitors that it leaves a new mother feeling she is playing to an audience which can affect the all important feeding and bonding process. By all means share this very special time with close family and friends, but remember that this first unforgettable month is your 'babymoon'; it can never be repeated and, above all, it is a time for you and your baby to enjoy.

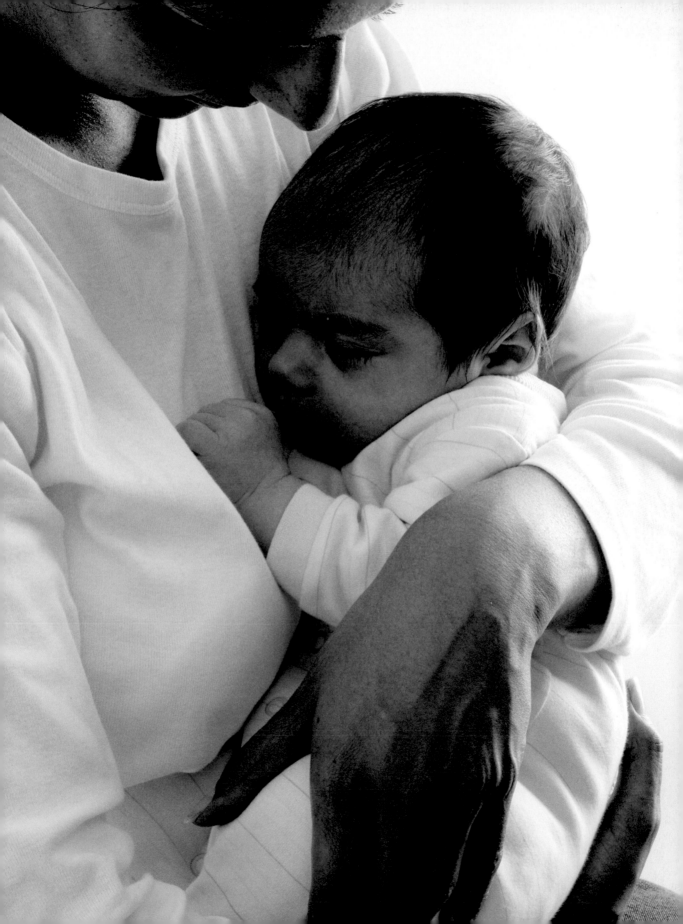

Feeding during the first month

Breast milk is without a doubt the best form of nourishment for your newborn baby. The World Health Organisation advises that all babies should be exclusively breastfed for at least six months and it is always worth trying to breastfeed in order to give your child the best possible start.

Establishing breastfeeding is not always easy, and does not come naturally for many mothers. Seeking advice from a recognised breastfeeding organisation such as the National Childbirth Trust or La Leche League (see page 234) will help get it off to a good start. It can take between six and eight weeks to establish a good milk supply and to see a regular pattern of feeding emerge.

> **TOP TIP**
>
> When breastfeeding, it is essential to look after yourself, to get as much rest as you can and to eat a healthy diet. It is also important to drink plenty of water as breastfeeding can be dehydrating and you may feel thirstier than usual.

A quiet time

During the early days of establishing breastfeeding, try to keep feed times as calm and quiet as possible. This will enable you to concentrate on getting the position right for you and your baby and to feel completely relaxed and comfortable.

Milk production

The 'let-down' reflex

Once your baby is put to the breast a hormone called oxytocin is released from the pituitary gland at the base of the brain, which sends a 'let-down' signal to the breast. The muscles supporting the milk glands contract and the milk is pushed down the milk ducts as the baby sucks. Many women feel a tingling sensation in their breasts and, in the early days, your womb may contract when the milk is let down. You may also experience the let-down reflex when you hear a baby cry or if you think about your baby when you are apart. Using breast pads will help soak up any milk leakage in between feeds.

Milk composition

The milk in your breasts is made up of two types: fore milk and hind milk. At the beginning of the feed your baby gets the fore milk, which is high in volume and low in fat. As the feed progresses, your baby's sucking will slow down and he will pause for longer between sucks. This is a sign that he is reaching the creamier hind milk. It is important that the baby is left on the breast long enough to reach it, as it is the high fat content of this milk that helps your baby go longer between feeds. If he is transferred to the second breast too soon, he will get two lots of fore milk which might leave him hungry again within an hour or two. It may also lead to him becoming very 'colicky'. In my experience, in the early days, babies who are allowed 25 minutes on the first breast before being offered the second go longer between feeds and colic can be avoided.

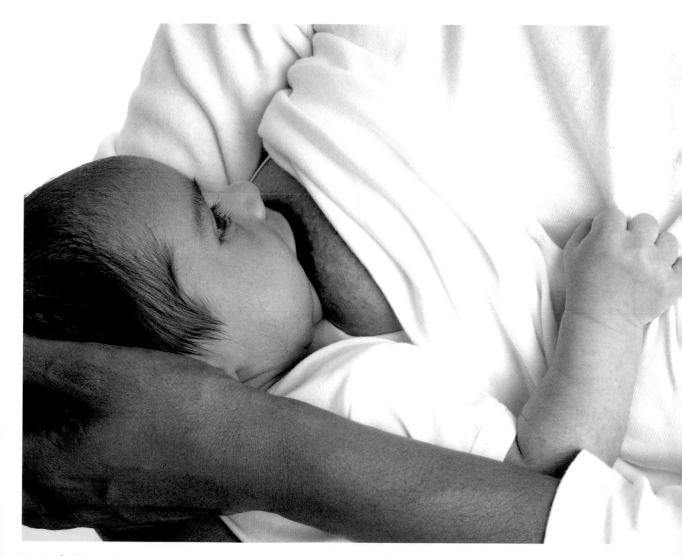

Keeping feed times calm and quiet will help you to concentrate on finding a breastfeeding position that is comfortable for you and your baby

Positioning

There are several different nursing positions; the one pictured on page 33 is the position that the majority of my mothers have used very successfully. However, if you have had a Caesarean section or a difficult birth, it would be advisable to ask your breastfeeding counsellor to help you find a position that is most comfortable for you.

- Good positioning is extremely important if the baby is to 'latch on' successfully.

- The baby needs to take your nipple and as much as possible of the areola (the brown area around it) into his mouth.

- Your nipple should be touching the roof of the baby's mouth and his lower lip should be rolled back against his chin.

- The baby should be able to suck hard without causing you any pain. If it hurts, ease him off gently and try again.

- It is essential to get the baby latched on properly if you are to breastfeed successfully, so it is really worth the effort to get the positioning right at the beginning. Good latching on will also mean that sore cracked nipples should not be a problem.

NURSING CHAIRS

The best type of seat for breast-feeding is one with a straight back. It should be reasonably wide and well upholstered. While rocking chairs are often recommended for breastfeeding, I find that the seats and arms are often not wide enough for the mother to get really comfortable and to arrange, if needed, cushions to support the baby. It is also tempting to rock back and forth, which can result in a baby who keeps dropping off to sleep during the feed.

Sitting comfortably

Whether you use a specially designed nursing pillow or several cushions will depend on many factors – the size of your baby, your breasts, and whether you are long in the waist or not. Experiment with different techniques during the early days until you find one that suits both you and your baby. The mothers I worked with found that having several differently sized cushions worked much better as they can be moved around and adjusted during the feed. Often, when a specially designed breastfeeding pillow is used, the baby remains in the same position throughout the feed, lying flat along the pillow and becoming very sleepy as a result. Not properly finishing the feed means that the baby often wakes up an hour later looking to be fed again.

Preparing for the feed

- Set out everything you need next to where you will be feeding well in advance. For example, a large glass of water and snack for yourself, along with tissues, muslin, bib, etc.

- It is important that your back is really straight during feeding. This is to prevent backache, which is a common problem when breastfeeding, and it will also help prevent future back problems. If need be, place a cushion or pillow behind your back for support.

- Place the side of your baby's head in the crook of your arm, and tuck the arm that is nearest your body around your side, in order to bring him closer to you. His tummy should be facing your tummy and his body should be slightly angled so that his head is higher than his tummy. This will help avoid trapped wind, which is more likely to happen if the baby is lying flat.

> **TOP TIP**
> Use different cushions under your arms and under your baby's bottom until you find a position that feels comfortable for both of you.

- His head should be close to your breast, but very slightly tilted back so that his nostrils are free to breathe.

- Use your free hand to support your breast, place your fingers under the breast, and your thumb on top, ensuring that they are all behind the areola.

- Bring your baby closer to you and use your nipple to gently stroke his upper lip until he opens his mouth .

- Once his mouth is open wide enough, gently place your nipple and the whole of the areola in the centre of his mouth so that he can latch on.

- If he is positioned properly on the breast, his bottom lip will curl out. If not, you will have to take him off and try again until he is latched on properly.

- To remove your nipple from your baby's mouth, break the suction firmly but gently by slipping your forefinger or little finger into the corner of his mouth and sliding it along until he releases it voluntarily. Do not attempt to pull your baby off the breast, as this can be very painful.

GETTING ENOUGH MILK

In the first weeks, some breastfeeding mothers become concerned that their baby is not getting enough milk, as, unlike bottle feeding, they cannot see exactly how much their baby is taking. Be guided by your baby; if he seems happy and is producing lots of wet nappies he is getting enough. If you are concerned that your baby seems constantly hungry and that you may not be producing enough milk to satisfy him, seek advice from a reputable breastfeeding counsellor. If you're still concerned, speak to your health visitor or doctor.

- Make sure that you are not leaning forward while your baby is on the breast, as this puts pressure on your back, which can lead to tension in your shoulders and arms and may affect your let-down reflex.

- When your baby has finished feeding you should use your thumb and forefinger to squeeze a little milk out of each breast and rub it around the nipple and areola. This will help prevent sore nipples. During the first month of breastfeeding it will also help if you can allow your nipples to air dry for 10–15 minutes after a feed.

Expressing milk

Breast milk is produced on a supply and demand basis. During the early days most babies will not need to feed from both breasts. By the end of the second week, milk production balances out and most mothers will be producing exactly the amount their babies are demanding. At some point during the third and fourth weeks the baby will go through a growth spurt and demand more milk and you may have to go back to feeding every two or three hours and often twice in the night in order to meet the increased demand. This pattern will be repeated every time the baby goes through a growth spurt. However, if you express milk from early on you will always be producing more milk than your baby needs. This means that when your baby has a growth spurt, your routine can stay intact because expressing less milk at the early-morning feeds means you will have enough to immediately satisfy your baby's increased appetite.

How to express

- The best time to express is in the morning as the breasts are usually fuller. The milk supply tends to become lower in the evening but milk can also be expressed at this time, in addition to the morning session.

- Expressing is easier if done at the beginning of a feed. Express one breast prior to feeding your baby or feed your baby from one breast, then express from the second breast before offering him the remainder of his feed.

- An electrical breast-pumping machine, the type used in hospitals, is by far the most effective way to express milk. The suction of these machines is designed to simulate a baby's sucking rhythm, encouraging the milk flow. These pumps can be hired from hospitals or through breastfeeding counsellors. You can also express using a hand or battery-operated pump, available from larger chemists. Breast pumps and bottles need to be washed and sterilised after every use (see page 41 for more on sterilising).

- In the early days you will need to allow at least 15 minutes to express 60–90ml (2–3oz) at the morning feed.

- Introducing a bottle of expressed milk for the 10pm feed by the second week will ensure that your baby will be happy to accept a bottle. Involving Dad at this feed will help them to bond and allow you time for some relaxation. The bottle is also important if you are thinking of returning to work in the future or if you would like someone else to feed your baby while you have a break.

- Breast milk can be stored in the fridge for 24 hours in a sterilised bottle or frozen in a sterilized bottle or bag for up to a month. Defrost and re-heat as formula milk.

> **TOP TIP**
> Massaging the breasts and having a warm bath or shower help stimulate the milk flow. Some mothers look at a photograph of their baby to encourage the flow.

Formula feeding

While breastfeeding is without a doubt the best way to feed your baby I appreciate that for some mothers this may not always be possible.

Whatever reason you have for formula-feeding your baby, it is important not to let other people's opinions influence how you feel about your decision or allow you to feel guilty. Formula milk has improved dramatically over the last few years, and thousands of formula-fed babies are growing up happily and healthily.

• The important thing when choosing a formula milk is to find one that is nearest in its make-up to breast milk.

• There are many different types of formula milk on the market, so go with first-stage milk, which is the nearest in composition to breast milk.

• Do not be tempted by second-stage milks for hungrier babies since the composition is different. By choosing a first-stage formula milk, and preferably an organic one, you will be giving your baby the next best thing to breast milk.

• You should take the same approach to feeding your baby as if you were breastfeeding. Do not try to implement a strict schedule, or try to make him go for four hours between feeds, as hospitals used to advise.

• Like the breastfed baby he should be woken and fed every three hours until he regains his birth weight.

• Once he has regained his birth weight, you should be able to establish a feeding pattern of approximately three hours between feeds during the day and a longer spell of four hours at night provided, of course, that your baby is taking the required amount for his age and weight. Should he not take the full amount and demand food sooner than three hours he should, of course, be fed.

Whatever reason you have for formula-feeding your baby, it is important not to let other people's opinions influence how you feel about your decision

Equipment

Bottles

If your baby is being exclusively formula-fed, you will need an assortment of 240ml (8oz) bottles and 120ml (4oz) bottles. I recommend wide-necked bottles as they are easier to fill and clean.

Teats

Most bottles come with slow-flow teats that are designed to meet the needs of newborns. By eight weeks I find that most babies feed better from medium-flow teats.

Cleaning

You will need a washing-up bowl solely for your bottles and teats, a bottle brush and sterilising equipment (see Cleaning and sterilising, page 41).

How much milk?

Health authorities advise that a baby less than four months old would need 70ml (2.5oz) of milk for each 450g (1lb) of his body weight; a baby weighing around 3.2kg (7lb) would need approximately 500ml (17oz) a day. This is only a guideline; hungrier babies may need an extra ounce at some feeds. The same guidelines apply as for breastfeeding: aim to get the baby to take most of his daily milk requirements between 7am and 11pm. This way he will only need a small feed in the middle of the night and will eventually drop it altogether.

In the first month, your baby may take anything from 60ml (2oz) to 150ml (5oz) per feed, depending on his size and appetite.

Overfeeding

Unlike the breastfed baby the most common problem in the early days with formula-fed babies is overfeeding. I believe this can happen when some babies take the bottle of formula so quickly that their natural sucking instincts are not satisfied and they end up screaming when the bottle is taken away. Many mothers interpret this as a cry of hunger and give another bottle of milk. A pattern of overfeeding can emerge, resulting in the baby gaining large amounts of weight each week. While it is normal for some babies to need an additional 30ml (1oz) at some feeds, special attention should be given if your baby is taking more than 150ml (5oz) at each feed and is regularly gaining more than 240g (8oz) of weight each week. Offering an ounce of cooled boiled water and/or a dummy may help satisfy a 'sucky' baby. If you are concerned that your baby is overfeeding, you should discuss the problem with your doctor or health visitor.

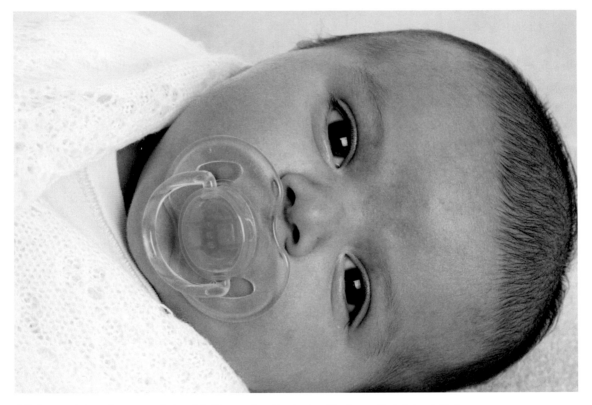

Offering your baby a dummy may help satisfy his natural sucking instinct if he is a particularly 'sucky' baby

Preparing the feed

When making up formula milk it is essential that you follow the instructions on the tin exactly. You will soon get into a routine of cleaning and sterilising bottles and making up feeds for the next 24 hours. Most of my mothers find that lunchtime, when the baby has gone for a nap, is a good time to do this. Once heated up, the feed should never be re-heated and any remaining milk should be discarded after an hour. If your baby requires a top-up feed, a fresh bottle of milk should be offered. In the early days it is a good idea to have an extra bottle of boiled water in the fridge for making up a quick extra bottle. Alternatively, ready-made formula can be bought in small cartons, ideal for taking out on trips or for use when you need milk quickly.

Cleaning and sterilising

The utmost attention must be paid to hygiene: the sterilising of all your baby's feeding equipment and the preparation and storage of formula milk.

- After each feed, the bottle and teat should be rinsed out thoroughly with cold water and put aside in a bowl. Fill the bowl with hot, soapy water and scrub all the dirty bottles, rims, caps and teats with a long-handled bottle brush, paying particular attention to the necks and rims. Carefully rinse everything under hot running water with a final cold rinse before sterilising.

- There are various methods of sterilising; equipment can be boiled in water for ten minutes in a sealed saucepan, steam sterilisers (electric or microwave) can be used or you can soak the bottles and equipment in a solution of water and special sterilising tablets. Always follow the manufacturer's instructions exactly regarding the day-to-day care of your steriliser.

The area where you prepare your baby's milk should be kept spotlessly clean

- The area where you prepare your baby's milk should be kept spotlessly clean. Hands should always be washed with anti-bacterial soap under warm running water then dried with kitchen roll, as tea towels are breeding grounds for germs.

Giving the feed

- As with breastfeeding, you will find that sitting in a straight-backed chair with arms is ideal.

- Use a cushion to support your back and place another under the arm you are supporting the baby with so that your baby is feeding in a position where his head is slightly higher than his tummy.

POSSETTING
It is very common for babies to bring up a small amount of milk while being burped, or after a feed. This is called possetting and for most babies it does not create a problem. A well-positioned muslin will usually catch whatever the baby brings up. However, if your baby is possetting excessively and not gaining weight, he could be suffering from a medical condition called 'reflux', in which case it is essential to get advice from your GP or health visitor.

- Have a bib and muslins ready.

- The milk needs only to be slightly warm; too warm and your baby will start to refuse the feed once it cools down.

- Check that the ring holding the teat and the bottle together is not too tight as it will restrict the flow of milk.

- Make sure the bottle is kept tilted up far enough to ensure the whole teat is always filled with milk. If the baby sucks air in through the teat this will give him wind.

- Allow him to continue feeding for as long as he wants before you burp him.

- He may take most of the feed, burp, have a break of 10–15 minutes and then finish the feed.

- In the first few weeks, allow up to an hour for a feed. As he gets older he will probably finish in about 20 minutes.

Winding baby

Regardless of whether your baby is breastfed or bottle-fed, it is best to allow him to take the lead when he needs to be winded. Let him take as much of the feed as he wants; you will probably find that midway during the feed he will pull himself off the breast or bottle and will need to be winded then.

The majority of babies will bring up their wind easily provided they are in the right position. I have often observed mothers spending 15–20 minutes trying to get their baby's wind up by constantly patting and rubbing their back, with both the mother and the baby getting more and more distressed. The baby may have difficulty in releasing the wind if he is sitting incorrectly.

- Sit your baby on your knee to wind him, supporting his head by placing your hand under his chin and across his chest.

- With your other hand, keep his back really straight and firmly stroke his back in an upward direction.

- If your baby hasn't burped after a few minutes, don't continue as he will only get distressed. Have a short break. Laying him flat for a few minutes then trying again often helps release the wind. Finish the feed, then wind him again.

It is best to allow your baby to take the lead when he needs to be winded

Support his head and body by placing your hand under his chin and across his chest, keeping his back totally straight

Sleeping

- Babies up to one month of age need approximately 16–18 hours of sleep a day, broken up into a series of short and long sleeps.

- Smaller babies and premature babies tend to need more sleep, and will be more likely to doze on and off between feeds.

- To avoid excessive night-time waking try to keep your baby awake for short spells after daytime feeds.

- I advise that a baby under one week needs approximately $5^{1}/_{2}$ hours sleep between the hours of 7am and 7pm, reducing to a maximum of 5 hours during the first month. This should be divided into three separate naps.

- To encourage your baby to sleep well at nap times during the day it is important that you structure his feeding.

- Sleeping and feeding are very closely linked in the early days, so it is important that he takes full feeds at the recommended times if he is to sleep well during his naptimes.

- During the first month fully swaddling your baby at naptimes will also help establish daytime naps.

Swaddling

The choice of swaddling blanket is important as the baby should not be able to wriggle out or overheat. Cotton cellular blankets are normally too small for effective swaddling and their thickness could cause overheating. Using a rectangular jersey cotton swaddle is best because the material is thin and stretchy and the shape is ideal for swaddling. It's easy to make two simple swaddles as follows:

- Take 2 metres (usually 140 cm wide) of stretch jersey cotton t-shirt fabric (available in department stores or haberdashers) cut into 2 x 1-metre lengths. Fold over the edge of the material twice for a 2 cm hem at the bottom and sides and a 4 cm hem at the top (for going around baby's neck).

- Effective swaddling will ensure that your baby cannot wriggle free. He will feel secure as he has his hands across his chest, but will also be able to move them around within the little pockets that you create. Practise on a large teddy 20 times or so, so that you can swaddle your baby really quickly.

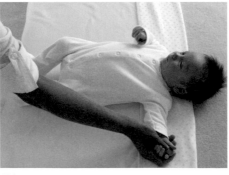
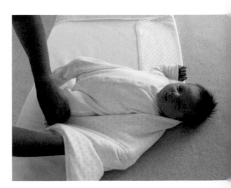

(a)   *(b)*   *(c)*

Contented swaddling

- Lay the swaddle on the floor or bed. Place baby to the right of centre on the blanket ensuring the top of the blanket is slightly higher than the back of his neck. *(a)*

- Take baby's left hand in your right hand, pointing it outwards from his body *(b)*, then with your left hand draw the right-hand side of the swaddle blanket across your baby's chest. Gently tug it downwards so the 4 cm border is sitting firmly around your baby's neck. *(c)*

- The baby's left hand and your right hand will now be under the swaddle material. Place your free hand on top of your baby's chest, which is now covered by a layer of swaddle material. Then, using your right hand, bring your baby's left hand across his chest, so that you have made a 'sleeve'. Tuck the excess blanket around his back and under his bottom. *(d)*

- Repeat the same procedure with your baby's right hand. Hold it up and outwards in your left hand, then with your right hand bring the remainder of the swaddling blanket across his chest *(e)*. Take the arm wrapped in the blanket across his chest, tucking the excess under his back and bottom.

Effective swaddling will help your baby feel secure as he has his hands across his chest

(d)

(e)

Establishing a good night-time sleep and bedtime routine

How your baby sleeps at night will depend very much on what happens during the day. As already mentioned in the feeding section, a small baby needs to feed little and often during the early days.

- If your baby is allowed to sleep for long stretches between feeds during the day, he will be more likely to wake more during the night needing to be fed.

- Waking and feeding your baby every three hours during the first month will mean that he will be much more likely to go his longer stretch in the night.

How your baby sleeps at night will depend very much on what happens during the day

- To ensure that this longer stretch is between 11pm and 6/7am, it is important that he sleeps well in the evening.

- Many parents think that keeping their baby awake for most of the evening will help them sleep longer in the night. I have rarely found that this is the case. More often than not, the baby is fretful and irritable and needs to feed on and off during the evening, then is so exhausted by 10pm that he only takes a small feed, waking again a couple of hours later.

- Because breast milk is produced on a supply and demand basis, a pattern of feeding every couple of hours can soon evolve.

- A baby whose daytime feeds and sleep have been structured, and who feeds well at 6pm and settles to sleep well between 7pm and 10pm will wake up refreshed and ready to take a full feed that will help him to sleep a longer stretch in the middle of the night.

The 7am to 7pm routine

I have tried many different routines over the years and, without exception, I have found the 7am to 7pm routine to be the one in which tiny babies and young infants are happiest, as it fits in with their natural sleep rhythms and their need to feed little and often. The aim of my sleeping and feeding advice is to settle your baby into a 7am to 7pm sleeping routine as soon as possible. The important thing to remember in the early days is that you are trying to achieve a regular sleeping pattern where your baby settles well in the evening, feeds and settles at 10.30pm, then only wakes once in the night for a feed and goes back to sleep quickly until 6/7am.

Napping

Young babies need three (sometimes four) naps during the day. As the routine becomes more established, the baby may nap in the buggy or car seat if you need to go out (see page 72).

The morning nap

Most babies are ready for a nap approximately two hours from the time they wake up in the morning. This should always be a short nap, around 45 minutes to one hour. Your baby should be gently woken after this time has lapsed.

The lunchtime nap

This should always be the longest sleep of the day and most babies will need a nap of two to two and a half hours. By establishing a good lunchtime nap you will ensure that your baby is not too tired to enjoy afternoon activities and that bedtime is relaxed and happy. Sleeping too long in the morning means that your baby will not sleep for long enough at lunchtime and he will become exhausted by the late afternoon. He will then need to go to bed much earlier than 7pm and may wake very early in the morning as a result.

Late afternoon nap

This is the shortest nap of the three and can be taken as a catnap in the pram or buggy, allowing you to be out and about. If you want your baby to go to sleep at 7pm do not let him sleep longer than 45 minutes and he should always be awake by 5pm, regardless of how long or short his nap was. From the age of three months onwards, most babies who are sleeping well at the other two naps will gradually cut back on this nap until it is no longer necessary.

The bedtime routine

It is never too early to start establishing a good bedtime routine, and even if your baby does not settle every evening for the length of time that I suggest, by being consistent and following the same routine every evening, you should find that by one month he is settling well between 7pm and 10pm. The following guidelines will help you establish a bath and bedtime routine that will encourage your baby to settle well at 7pm.

- Try to ensure that your baby is awake for short spells after daytime feeds, and that after he is one week old, his total daily nap time is no more than five hours between 7am and 7pm.

- Keep a diary of your baby's feeds during the day so that if he doesn't settle well you may be able to trace the reason why from your notes.

- Keep the bedtime routine calm and quiet. Dim the lights and avoid lots of talking and eye contact during the last feed.

Settling your baby

When settling your baby at sleep times I would advise that you use the same holding positions each time. By using the same technique your baby will soon start to associate it with falling asleep. Many babies get very distressed when they suddenly go from the warmth of their parents' chest and arms to being on their back, alone in the cot. The settling technique shown opposite will help make the transition from your arms to the cot much easier for your baby.

- Holding your baby across your chest (a), will help him feel calm and secure, and also prevent him thrashing his arms and legs around if he is fretful.

- Once he is calm and his breathing is steady you should move him to the crook of your arm, but continue to hold his hands across his chest (b).

- After a minute or two you can let go of one of his hands, a minute or two later let go of the second. The aim is to have his whole body in a relaxed, sleepy state as shown (c), but settled in his cot before he actually goes to sleep.

Sleep rhythms and sleep associations

Between the third or fourth week your baby becomes more alert and will be less likely to fall into a deep sleep straight away after feeding. This is often a

(a)

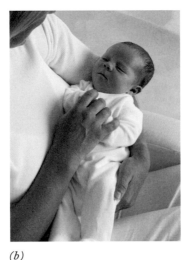
(b)

(c)

time when the wrong sleep associations develop as parents may resort to feeding, rocking or patting their baby to induce sleep. They do not realise that this is the age when the different stages of sleep become more apparent.

Like adults, babies drift from light sleep into a dream-like sleep known as REM sleep, then into a deep sleep known as non-REM. Their sleep cycle is much shorter than that of an adult, lasting approximately half an hour to 45 minutes. While some babies simply stir when they drift into light sleep, others wake up fully. If the baby is due a feed this does not create a problem. However, if this is not the case, and the baby is 'helped' back to sleep by some other method, this can create a real problem over the months ahead as your baby will not be able to drift back into sleep without help from you. If you want your baby to develop good sleep habits from an early age it is important not to allow the wrong sleep associations to develop. Always settle your baby before he falls asleep. This will help him learn to fall asleep independently at sleep times.

- Babies under six weeks have a strong Moro (startle) reflex so make sure he is swaddled very securely or he may wake himself up with a sudden movement.

- Hunger, especially with breastfed babies, is one of the main causes of young babies not settling in their cots. If, after 5–10 minutes, he is getting very upset, offer him more to eat. Resettle him and leave him another 5–10 minutes. If he is still very unsettled, repeat the procedure. You may have to repeat this several times before he eventually falls asleep.

- If this pattern continues for more than a few nights it is possible your milk supply is low at this time and it would be advisable to offer him a top-up of expressed milk to eliminate the problem.

The bed and bathtime routine

I firmly believe that incorporating a bath and a massage into your bedtime routine will help your baby settle better, and there has been some research that supports my belief that babies who are bathed and massaged every day in the evening tend to sleep better than those that aren't. I think that babies are no different to us and I am sure that one of your pleasures in life is a lovely warm soak at the end of a long day. Of course your baby may not always need a bath, but by giving him one every evening you can be sure that he feels fresh and clean as well as relaxed. The following guidelines will help ensure that bath time is a calm and relaxing occasion.

- Never attempt to bath a baby who is tired, hungry and getting near his feed. Until he nears eight weeks, give him half of his feed at 5pm after his afternoon nap, followed by a kick without his nappy, then his bath. The rest of the feed can be given after the bath, but ensure that he is feeding no later than 6.15pm.

- Prepare everything in advance for the bath, making sure that you have towels, nightclothes, creams and anything else you might need laid out ready.

- Close the curtains or blinds and lower the lighting. Make sure that both the bedroom and bathroom are warm enough as young babies feel the cold more than adults.

- Always fill the bath with cold water first and then add the hot water. The water needs to be warm but not too hot. Test the temperature with your wrist or elbow as these are more sensitive to heat than your hands. Do not add any bubble bath or bath oil at this stage.

How to bath your baby

- Undress your baby, remove his nappy and clean his bottom before wrapping him securely in a large towel.

- At this age always wash your baby's face and neck separately before you bath him, using cotton wool dampened in some cooled boiled water. Use two

Make sure that both the bedroom and bathroom are warm enough as young babies feel the cold more than adults

small separate pads of cotton wool to wipe his eyes, always wiping from the inside corner of his eye to the outside. Always dry your baby's face with a clean face flannel.

- Holding your baby in the 'football hold', lean over the bath and rinse his head and hair off with the clean bath water. Once you have done this you can then add some mild baby bath wash.

- Unwrap your baby and place the towel within easy reach for when you take him out of the bath. Lower your baby into the bath, position the bath and yourself so that he has close contact with you and doesn't lose sight of your face. A young baby can only see to a distance of 20–30 cm.

- Using a special baby bath support within the bath allows you to have both hands free. If your baby thrashes his arms and gets upset, you can then hold both his hands across his chest with one of your hands to calm him down.

- If your baby is a bit fretful, talk to him in a calm voice, explaining step by step which bits of his body you are washing, etc. Remember, he will sense if you are anxious, so try to reassure him in a positive tone.

- Allow him no longer than 5–10 minutes even if he seems to love his bath. He will get very tired once he is out of the bath, and it is important that you allow enough time for massaging and dressing, so he is not overtired for the feed.

> **SAFETY**
> It is very important that you never leave your baby unsupervised in the bath, not even for a second. Young children and babies can very easily drown in shallow water and tragic accidents happen every year because parents have left the room for a moment to answer the telephone, or to fetch a towel. Always have everything to hand before you start the bath, and never be distracted by doorbells ringing or other disturbances.

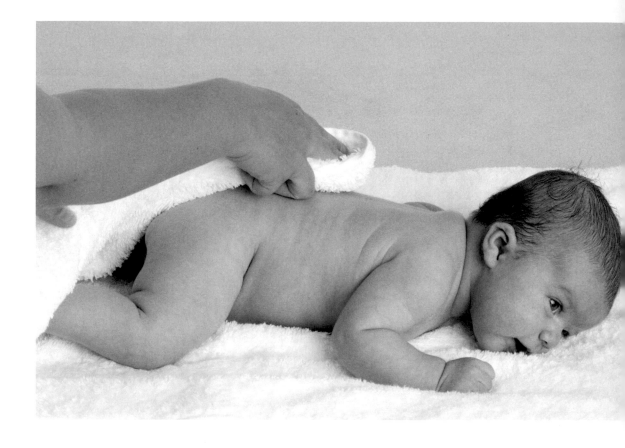

- Lift your baby out of the bath, remembering to say, 'Up you come', then wrap him firmly in his towel and take him quickly through to the nursery. Sit him on your lap and dry the front of his body with the towel before you lay him on the changing mat.

- Then lay him down on his tummy with his head to one side and dry the back of his body. By doing it in this order you ensure that the towel you lay him down on does not get too wet.

Massaging your baby

- The room should be warm, around 25°C (77°F), and your baby laid on a warm soft towel or mat. Make sure your hands are nice and warm by rubbing them together well with a little oil before you begin.

- You can use one of the natural organic baby oils or baby lotion. Avoid nut-based oils, such as almond oil.

• Using a small amount of oil or lotion, and with gentle strokes, start at the back of your baby's shoulders and massage him all over.

• Turn him onto his front and again, starting at the top of his shoulders, gently massage his front and arms. Avoid the tummy area in babies under one month old. Many babies get upset when their tummies are exposed to the air; draping a muslin over their tummy will help them feel more secure.

• He may start to get a little fretful by this time, as he will be getting hungry, so try to work quickly when dressing him. Once he is dressed and ready for his feed wrap a big muslin around his neck to ensure that his clean nightclothes do not need to be changed should he possett just prior to being put down.

• Massaging your baby should be a relaxing and enjoyable experience for both of you. However, if your baby seems distressed, stop the massage and try again another day.

Safe sleeping

It is up to you whether you use a full-size cot, a Moses basket or a small crib for your baby's sleeptimes in the early days. I personally think it is a good idea for your baby to get used to the big cot from a young age even if you are using a Moses basket for most of the sleeps, but some parents prefer the portability of a Moses basket, which can be placed next to their bed at night. Whichever you prefer, your baby should always be put down to sleep on his back, as research has found this to be the most effective way of guarding against SIDS (Sudden Infant Death Syndrome), also known as cot death.

Your baby should always be put down to sleep on his back

Safety guidelines

• Your baby's head should never be covered up when sleeping. If your baby is in the big cot always ensure that he is placed in the 'feet to foot' position, with his toes right at the end of the cot. This will prevent him working his way down the cot while sleeping and accidentally getting his head under the blankets.

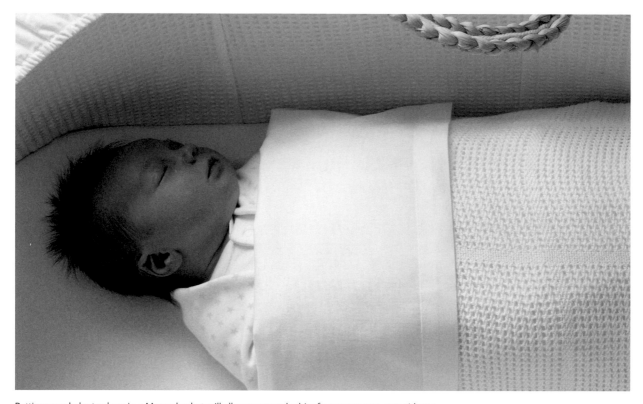

Putting your baby to sleep in a Moses basket will allow you to take him from room to room with you

- Tuck blankets and sheets in well so that your baby cannot get his head under the covers. A small rolled-up towel on either side of the baby between the mattress and the bars will help secure the blankets and sheets.

- Quilts and duvets are not recommended for babies under one year old as they can cause overheating.

- Depending on the temperature of the room, remember to adjust your baby's clothing and the layers of bedding. Be sure to count the swaddling sheet or blanket as one of the layers.

- The Foundation for the Study of Infant Deaths recommends that the room temperature is between 16 and 20°C (60-68°F). It is worthwhile investing in a good electronic room thermometer to measure this.

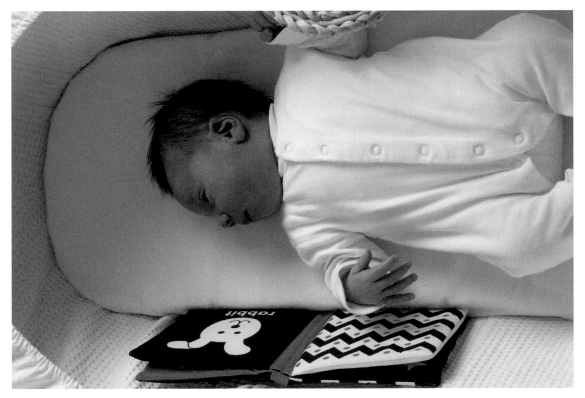

Have a variety of different books to prop inside his Moses basket to entertain him during his awake periods but make sure you remove them at sleep times

Poor sleepers

All babies are different and while some are good sleepers, many are fretful and difficult to settle. If your baby is one of the latter, please take heart as this need not be a reflection of your baby's future sleep habits. Be patient, consistent and allow time for good sleep routines to be established.

It is also important to remember that not all babies begin to sleep through the night at the same age. The majority of babies that I have helped care for usually started to sleep from the 10pm feed through to 6–7am somewhere between eight and 12 weeks. A few slept through before that age and some needed to be fed in the night for much longer. By following my guidelines, and adjusting the routines if need be to suit your particular child, he will sleep the longest spell at night as soon as he is physically and mentally capable of doing so.

Development

Every baby is unique. Babies develop at differing rates, and the month-by-month development that I describe is based on the acknowledged development rate of an average child. However, each baby has its own pattern and I always reassure mothers that while it is helpful to know what an average baby's development should be, comparisons with other babies are irrelevant and can often produce needless anxiety. From my experience of working with many babies over the years, I know that each of the developmental milestones is reached with varying degrees of speed, and at the right stage for your baby. No two babies are the same and it should be noted that if your baby was born prematurely it is likely that his development will be slower than that of a full-term baby.

Your baby's senses

- Babies quickly learn to recognise their mother's voices and it is thought that a baby becomes familiar with the intonation of his mother's voice while in the womb. Talk gently to your newborn baby, and use your voice to settle him. Singing and humming can be very soothing for your baby, and a good way to settle a newborn infant. It also encourages communication skills.

- A newborn baby is born with a strong sense of smell and quickly learns to recognise the smell of his own mother.

Singing and humming can be very soothing for your baby

- Your newborn baby is very sensitive to his surroundings and will respond to noise very soon after birth. A baby is most relaxed in a quiet room, with subdued lighting and the familiarity of the voices and handling of those he is getting to know as his family.

- As your baby's hearing develops, his ability to be able to turn towards a noise will be increasing. He will also begin to react to the noises around him and may become distressed by loud noises or disturbances or, alternatively, soothed by the voices of those with whom he is most familiar.

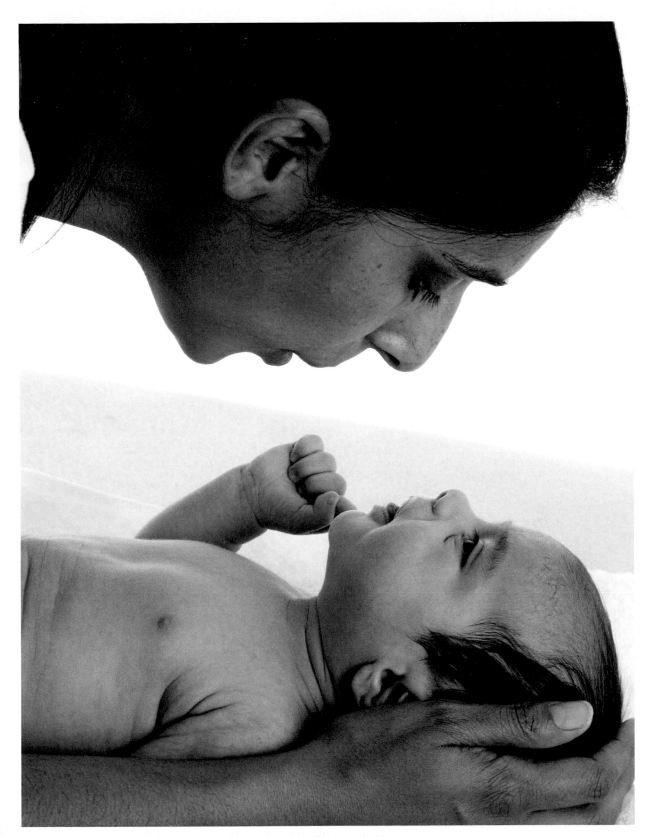

Your baby will love the sound of your voice so talking to him softly will help soothe him

- Most babies are able to cry loudly from birth. It is this first cry that reassures both the parents and the midwife that the baby is taking his first breath in the world. Crying is the most effective means for your baby to communicate with you. The most usual reason for a baby to cry is to tell you he is hungry. Your baby will also communicate by crying if he is tired, cold, lonely or in any kind of pain or discomfort. One of the most reassuring developments for a mother is learning to understand her baby's cry.

- The eyes of a newborn baby are light sensitive. He has been cradled in a warm, dark womb for nine months, and it takes time for him to adjust to the bright lights of a hospital or bedroom. It is soothing for a newborn baby to have subdued lighting while his eyes adjust to his new world.

Physical development

- It is not unusual for a very young baby's eyes to appear to be looking in different directions. By the end of the first month, he will have learnt to co-ordinate his eye movement more.

- Your baby's eye colour may change during the first six weeks, although it may not be permanently developed until your child is six months old.

YOUR BABY'S VISION
At birth your baby's ability to see is limited to people or objects within 20–30 cm. It is thought that it is easier for a baby to focus on black and white images but he will also show a particular interest in looking at faces.

- Your baby is born with a complete set of taste buds. He will naturally prefer the sweetness of breast milk, but will quickly become used to other flavours that are apparent in his mother's milk.

- A newborn baby has little head control due to the weakness in his neck muscles,

It is soothing for a newborn baby to have subdued lighting while his eyes adjust to his new world

so he will be reliant on you to support his head and neck when being lifted. By the end of the first month, your baby will probably be able to lift his head very briefly when lying on his stomach.

Physical reflexes

At birth, your baby demonstrates a number of different reflexes, which indicate a developing nervous system. The nerves of a newborn baby are unformed, and as the nerve connections develop, your baby's motor-neurone skills improve.

HICCUPS

Hiccups are common in newborn babies and it is not unusual for a baby to sound rather laborious in his breathing, as he is learning to breathe through his nose. As his nasal passage becomes bigger, the snuffling noise will begin to diminish.

Rooting and suckling reflex

Your baby is born with the reflex to root and suckle. For most babies, being placed on their mother's tummy or at her breast triggers the rooting reflex. Your baby will turn his head in a quest to find a nipple. The feeling of his mother's nipple in the roof of his mouth stimulates the sucking reflex. He will naturally suckle and swallow, and has a natural reflex to gag if the milk supply is too fast.

Walking reflex

If you hold your baby upright on a flat surface, he may appear to take a step with his foot, raising one leg and then the other. This walking reflex may last until the third month, and then begins to fade as your baby learns to control his reflexes. There is also something called the tonic reflex which a newborn baby demonstrates by turning his head to one side and extending an opposite arm to leg. Not all babies will demonstrate these reflexes as clearly as others, and it is important not to worry if you think your baby is not showing signs of them. Speak to your doctor or your health visitor if you have any concerns regarding your baby's development. In most instances you will find that your baby has been tested for these reflexes, and you will be reassured to find that his response is normal.

Moro reflex

Your baby will also display the 'Moro' reflex that will usually occur when he is disturbed by a sudden movement or noise. He will appear to 'start'

GRASPING AND CLENCHING

If you present your baby with a finger to hold, he will naturally grasp it. His hold can be surprisingly strong. Lightly stroking the palms or backs of your baby's hands or the sole of his feet will encourage him to uncurl his fingers or toes. These naturally stay quite tightly clenched in the early weeks. He may also enjoy having the soles of his feet massaged – this can have a very calming effect on some babies.

involuntarily and will fling out his arms and legs as if to protect himself.

Don't be alarmed by the jerkiness of this reflex. It is quite normal, and your baby will gradually grow out of it as he learns to control his muscle movement.

Encouraging your baby's development

The pleasure you are able to show in your baby's skills naturally encourages your baby. Whether it is talking in a singsong voice, smiling, repeating gurgling noises or simply making regular eye contact, the close interaction strengthens the bond between you and your baby and stimulates his mental development. You may find that this type of behaviour comes naturally but some parents may be more inhibited and take longer to feel confident and relaxed with their infant.

It is possible, however, to overstimulate a young baby with too much interaction. Your baby will be most responsive to interaction when he is rested.

Tummy time

One of the ways in which you can help your baby's physical development from the earliest days is to lie him on his tummy for a short time each day. This position will help him to gain head and neck control, learn to begin to take the weight of his upper body on to his arms and, finally, prepare him for crawling. Medical research has shown that the most effective way to protect your baby from cot death (see page 53) is to place him to sleep on his back.

- In order that your baby does not get used to only being on his back, it is helpful to encourage your baby to spend some time on his tummy when he is awake, to help him get him used to this position.

- In the first few weeks, try putting your baby on his tummy when you are changing or dressing him.

- The firm surface of the changing mat beneath him will give him support. To begin with, he may just lie with his head to one side, but very soon he will attempt to lift it up and possibly turn to face the other way.

- Your baby will only be able to hold his head up for a second or two in the beginning but each time he is placed on his tummy he will be gaining better head control and upper-body strength.

- Place a colourful toy or book in front of him to encourage him to look up.

- If your baby seems to dislike this position, don't give up; instead, let him lie on his tummy on his play mat with a rolled towel under his chest. Or he may prefer to lie prone on your chest when you are sitting well back in a comfortable chair, so he can lift his head to look at you as you talk or sing to him.

Encouraging development through play

By the age of four weeks most babies are happy to amuse themselves for short periods after they have fed. At this stage the thing your baby will love most is to listen to your voice and study your face. When he is awake, get him used to sitting in his chair for short periods; as long as he knows you are close enough, he should not become fretful. During the first four weeks, when your baby is awake, encourage him to become familiar with his nursery and a few different toys. However, do not overstimulate him with too many toys at this age.

Close interaction strengthens the bond between you and your baby and stimulates his mental development

- Babies gradually 'uncurl' during the first month and you should encourage your baby regularly to spend 10–15 minutes under the playgym. Prop black and white or brightly coloured books, especially ones with faces on them, around the pram or cot when he is awake. Some baby books have bold contrasting pictures in black, white and red on one side and a wider variety of colours and pictures on the reverse, which means they will be useful for several months as your baby's fine vision improves.

- Before the bath, and in a warm room, remove your baby's clothes and nappy. Then lay him on a changing mat on the floor, with some brightly coloured toys or books to look at, so he can have a good kick.

- By the end of the first month you may hear your baby make small cooing sounds. Encourage him to vocalise more by repeating the sound back to him. This is a very early stage in making conversation. He may also try to imitate your facial movements when you hold him close and talk to him by opening and closing his mouth. Encourage this by pausing to give him time to 'reply' to you.

- By the third or fourth week your baby may enjoy looking at a musical cot mobile. Some of these are angled so that the objects appear and disappear from his range of vision, encouraging him to track them with his eyes. If your baby seems upset by the music and movement, wait another week or so. Just let him look at the objects hanging above him without the sound and movement.

TOP TIP
Talk to your baby about what you are doing, especially when dressing and bathing him. He will love the sound of your voice and, with eye contact as well, it may help him become less distressed by being dressed and undressed.

- Your baby will enjoy a brightly coloured rattle shaken gently above him, or to one side. This too will encourage him to move his head to see where the sound is coming from.

Your baby may also try to imitate your facial movements when you hold him close and talk to him by opening and closing his mouth; encourage this by pausing to give him time to 'reply' to you

Q&A

newborns

Q

My baby's scalp is covered in yellowish scales and her forehead and the areas behind her ears are starting to look very dry and irritated. My mother suggested that I use a special shampoo for cradle cap, but I am a bit concerned about all the chemicals that seem to be in the shampoo.

A

Cradle cap, also called seborrhoeic dermatitis, is very common in small babies. It is caused by hormonal changes that stimulate secretions from the oil glands in the skin. I usually find that rubbing a small amount of olive oil on to the baby's scalp for 20 minutes or so before the bath, then gently massaging the scalp with a warm damp facecloth helps remove the scales. The hair and scalp can then be washed with a mild baby shampoo. Doing this on a regular basis and ensuring that you always rinse your baby's scalp with fresh clean warm water (not the water that she is being bathed in) will help keep it under control. Brushing your baby's hair gently with a very soft baby hairbrush every day, will also help keep the scalp clean and healthy.

Q

How do I keep my baby's navel clean until his umbilical cord drops off?

A

The stump should simply be cleaned regularly with cooled boiled water and cottonwool, then dried with a piece of dry cotton wool. When putting on your baby's nappy, be sure to fold it below the stump so that it is exposed to the air and not to urine. Avoid bathing your baby until the area heals completely and the stump falls off. When it does so, you may detect a little blood on the nappy, which is normal. If you are concerned about the condition of the stump, do consult your doctor.

Q

My baby is nearly three weeks old and I have been trying to establish some sort of feeding and sleeping routine. She is very sleepy during the day and can only stay awake for 30–40 minutes at the most, sometimes less. She goes down for all of her daytime naps and would sleep all day if I let her. But come the evening she is a different baby. She's had one night of not really settling for more than 45 minutes at a time, that lasted 12 hours! Last night, she wouldn't settle until after the 10pm feed and then was awake on and off for nearly seven hours, not sleeping properly until 5am this morning. I am offering her a feed each time she wakes, but this makes no difference in getting her to sleep. We are trying to stick to the same bedtime routine each evening, with a bath at 5.45pm and a quiet feed after the bath.

Why can she settle and sleep so well during the day but can't in the evening? How can I change this without leaving her to cry herself to sleep?

A

All babies are different in how much sleep they need. During the first month some will feed, stay awake for a short period then settle easily and sleep until the next feed. If they do this both day and night they are clearly a baby who needs more sleep. However, when a baby settles into a pattern like your baby has of sleeping well during the day, and not sleeping well at night, there are usually only three reasons. The first is hunger, the second is overtiredness and the third is too much daytime sleep.

Because you always offer your baby a feed each time she is unsettled and her weight gain is good, I feel that you can rule out hunger. Because she is sleeping so much during the day I also think that you can rule out overtiredness. I am fairly sure that too much daytime sleep is the reason your baby does not settle in the evening and wakes so much in the night. When this happens a vicious circle soon emerges where the baby needs to sleep more during the day because they are not sleeping well at night.

In my experience the only way to reverse this with such a small baby is to assist the baby to sleep in the evening for several nights. It should only take a few nights of getting her to sleep between 7pm and 10pm and then she would be easier to keep awake more in the mornings, which in turn would have a knock on effect of her sleeping better in the evening. By constantly picking your baby up and down and resettling with the dummy you are creating a worse sleep association than if you assist her to sleep for a few nights.

Assisting her to sleep will mean that for the first two or three nights you use the settling procedure as described on page 48–49, but instead of putting her in the moses basket you continue to hold her for a good two to three hours. Obviously you have to make sure that you are in a comfortable seat to do this, and it is important that the same person does the holding for the whole time. Passing her from person to person or continu-

ally picking her up from the moses basket actually causes more problems than holding her for a few nights. Once she has done a few nights of sleeping more than two hours in your arms you can then settle her in the moses basket, but keep her right next to you so that you can reassure her if she stirs.

While you are doing this in the evening, it is also important to alter her daytime sleep slightly until her sleep in the evening and night sleep becomes more consistent. When she gets tired at 8am, instead of putting her in her cot to until 10am, allow her a short nap in her bouncy chair or buggy of 20–30 minutes,then give her a urther short nap at around 10.30/10.45am of 15 minutes. This would make a total nap time of no more than 45 minutes between and 8am and 10am, reducing her morning sleep considerably. Allow

her a good two- to three- hour nap at lunchtime but then instead of letting her sleep from 3pm to 5pm in the afternoon, allow her two shorter naps of 20–30 minutes at around 3pm and 4.30pm. While you are following the recommended sleep times you may have to give her additional top-up milk feeds so that she is happy between sleep times. If you are consistent you should find that within a week she is sleeping well between 7pm and 10pm. When this happens it is iimportant that you have her awake properly between 10 and 11pm so that she feeds well then, settles to sleep easily and goes a reasonable time in the night before needing to feed. Gradually as her nightime sleep improves, you should find it easier to keep her awake for longer during the day after feeds, allowing you to revert back to proper scheduled naps times.

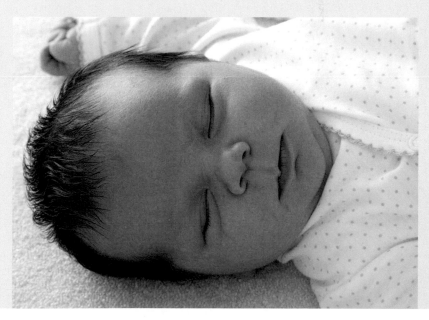

The
Second
Month

THE START OF THE SECOND MONTH SEES AN END TO THE 'BABY MOON' period, and life begins to return to normal. Of course, normal life with a baby will not be quite the same as the normal life you had before he arrived. During the first month everything usually revolves around the baby's feeding and sleeping needs. But during the second month, feeding times may begin to get shorter as your baby becomes more efficient at feeding. A pattern of regular sleep times should begin to evolve, and hopefully you will find that he is sleeping at least one longer spell in the day and one at night. These changes in your baby's feeding and sleeping patterns will now allow you to get out and about for longer than was probably possible during the first month. This is also a good time to look at establishing regular meetings with other parents. This is particularly important if you do not have family living close by who can give you the emotional and practical support that is so important in the early months. If you have spent years of working in a lively and exciting environment, being at home all day with the baby can be lonely at times so try to get out of the house every afternoon, whether it is for a walk to the park with another parent or going along to the local baby and toddler group.

Establishing a daily routine

During the second month you should start to see a regular pattern of feeding and sleeping emerge. Try to set up a daily routine that works for both you and your baby. For example, after the morning feed, you could get him used to lying on his play mat or sitting in his bouncy chair while you take a shower.

After the 10am feed, encourage him to have a little kick under his playgym while you quickly do the essential chores. If you establish this pattern now, then months down the line you will not become exhausted and frustrated because your baby needs to be held and entertained every minute of the day.

Taking a break

Now is a good time, if you have not already done so, to arrange for someone else to care for your baby for a short spell. I have found that the longer a mother puts this off, the harder it becomes. As long as you choose someone that you trust and who is familiar with young babies, it will do both you and

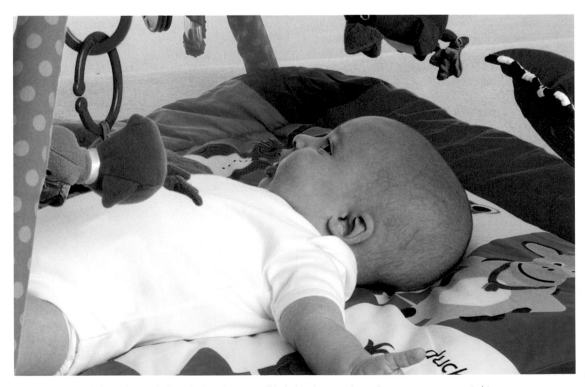

Encouraging your baby to have a kick under his playgym will help him become less reliant on you to entertain him

your baby good to spend an hour or two apart. Try to do something for yourself, whether it is having a relaxing massage or simply going for a coffee and reading the newspaper. A little bit of pampering for Mummy is very important in the early days!

The first time you choose to leave your baby with someone, try to arrange for them to come to your house. Ideally, they should already have spent time with you looking after the baby under your supervision so that they are familiar with the way you like things done for your baby. Remember, it is your baby so do not feel awkward about leaving them written instructions on how to deal with him while you are out.

Feeding

- Your baby will hopefully have established a more regular feeding pattern of five to six feeds between 7am and 10.30pm. If you find that your baby is not sleeping well at the lunchtime nap, it would be advisable to offer him a top-up feed prior to settling him. If he refuses this and wakes up after 45 minutes or so and does not settle back to sleep within 5–10 minutes, I would advise that you offer him a short feed to try and get him back to sleep. Treat this feed like a night feed and try and settle your baby back to sleep.

- You should find that he is now able to sleep for a longer spell in the night, provided he is getting most of his required milk intake between 7am and 10.30pm.

- He should still continue to have a regular weight gain of approximately 170g 225g(6-8 oz) per week. However, if your baby is putting on less than this amount, have a chat with your GP or health visitor who can reassure you as to whether or not you need to be concerned. The important thing they will want to check is whether your baby is happy, thriving and sleeping well.

Is your baby getting enough milk?

If your baby is not settling well at nap times and not sleeping longer in the night, and gaining less than the recommended amount of weight, he is probably not getting enough to eat at some or all of his feeds. If you are breastfeeding you may have to offer him both breasts at each feed. If you are already doing this it could be that you have a low milk supply and I would advise that for a week or so you put your baby to the breast more often to help increase the amount of milk you are producing. Try offering your baby the breast prior to nap times as this will not only help him sleep better, but the extra sucking will help produce more milk. You will find a more detailed plan on how to increase your milk supply in *The Contented Little Baby Book*. I would also advise that you seek guidance from a professional breastfeeding counsellor to ensure that you are getting your baby positioned on the breast correctly. Poor positioning on the breast is one of the main causes of young babies not feeding properly, which in turn affects the amount of milk produced. If your baby is formula-fed, talk to your health visitor if he is not gaining enough weight so they can advise you on whether you are giving him enough at each feed.

The six-week growth spurt

- Most babies go through a growth spurt at around six weeks of age, and yours may want to increase his daytime milk intake at this stage.

- He may need to go back to feeding slightly longer at all or some of his feeds for a few days, or have a short top-up breastfeed prior to naps.

- If you have established a regular routine of expressing milk, you can reduce the amount you are expressing at your morning feeds, so that your baby gets more milk at these feeds.

- You could also give him a top-up bottle of expressed milk after his night-time feed, if you think your supply has become low at the end of the day.

- A formula-fed baby should have the amount he is taking increased by 30 ml (1oz) if he is regularly draining his bottles at each feed.

- Do not forget to look after yourself, particularly if you are breastfeeding your baby. To ensure that you have a good milk supply and do not become overtired, it is very important that you have at least three good meals a day and healthy snacks in between, that you drink lots of fluids and that you try to have a rest in the middle of the day.

Sleeping

The big cot

During the second month, I would advise you to put your baby in his big cot for some of his sleep time (if you've not already done so) in order that he can become familiar with this environment. You should also begin to get him used to being half-swaddled at some of his sleep times (see below). Remember to put your baby in the cot while he is sleepy, but still awake, and then allow him to settle himself to sleep. If he gets into the habit of being held, rocked or fed to sleep, there is a chance that the wrong sleep associations will set in.

Moving to half-swaddling

By the age of six weeks you should be getting your baby used to being only half-swaddled at his sleep times. Cot death rates peak between two and four months and overheating is thought to be a major factor. Swaddle the baby as usual but wrap the swaddle cloth under both his arms, instead of over the arms.

It is really important that you follow the medical advice on guarding against cot death by placing your baby to sleep on his back, and with his feet almost touching the bottom of the cot, so he cannot slide under the covers.

Remember to adjust the number of layers of bedding according to the temperature of the room, as described on page 54.

Sleeping at night

During the second month, if you want to encourage your baby to sleep longer in the night, it is important that you watch the amount of sleep he has during the day. I usually recommend a maximum of $4^{1}/_{2}$ hours sleep at one month between the hours of 7am and 7pm, reducing to a maximum of 4 hours by the end of two months. This should be divided up into three separate naps and your baby should be either half- or fully swaddled when he goes down for his naps. By the end of the second month your baby's sleep cycle will become more defined, alternating between light sleep and deep sleep, sometimes referred to as REM sleep and non-REM sleep. He will start to come into a light sleep every 30 or 40 minutes, before drifting back into a deep sleep.

As before, to encourage him to sleep well at night-time, it is important to make sure the room is darkened and that you do not talk to him or have eye contact while he is settling down to sleep. When it is time for him to wake up, turn the lights on, un-swaddle him and allow him to wake up naturally in his cot before picking him up.

Naps and going out

Now is a good time to ensure that some of his daytime naps are taken in the buggy or baby chair. It is important that he learns to sleep elsewhere so that life is not too restricted as he gets older, and you can both enjoy days out with family and friends.

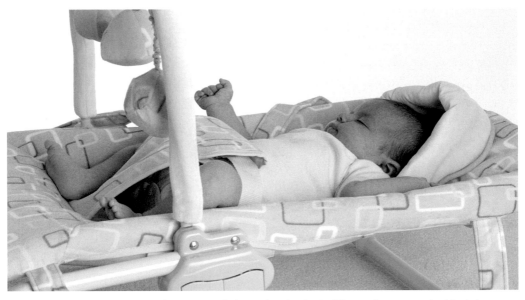

Visiting friends can be made easier if you get your baby used to sleeping in different places – try using his chair

The bed and bathtime routine

Continue with the established bathtime and bedtime routine, though your baby may now be staying slightly longer in the bath. He should be starting to look at and take an interest in any bath toys that you introduce.

Immunisation

When your baby is two months old you will be asked to take him to your local surgery or health centre for vaccination. This is the start of a programme of baby immunisation that, in the first year, is given in three stages – at the age of two, three and four months. You should keep a record of these vaccinations (most health authorities provide you with a record book) as well as ensuring that your child completes the entire course of immunisation.

At two months, a DTaP/IPV/Hib injection will be offered which protects against five different diseases: diphtheria, tetanus, pertussis (whooping cough), polio and haemophilus influenzae type b (Hib). Hib is an infection that causes a number of illnesses such as pneumonia and meningitis. However, this immunisation only protects infants from the Hib form of meningitis. You should also be aware that it does not protect them from other types, such as viral and meningococcal meningitis.

Your baby will also be given a vaccination known as PCV. This protects against pneumococcal infection, which can cause diseases such as septicaemia and meningitis.

Concerns

Having your baby vaccinated can be an upsetting experience for many parents. You will be asked to hold your baby while the injection is taking place and he will probably cry during the procedure, as well as for a short time afterwards. Try to comfort yourself with the thought that your baby will soon have forgotten all about it and that you are protecting him.

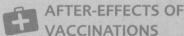

TOP TIP
For a full schedule of childhood immunisation and more information on the various vaccinations, go to www.immunisation.org.uk.

AFTER-EFFECTS OF VACCINATIONS

All babies react differently to vaccines and some are not affected at all. Others may develop a slight temperature and can become quite irritable and restless. In these cases, baby paracetamol can be given. Be sure to follow the instructions regarding the measurements for the age group exactly, or ask the nurse administering the injection for advice. Your baby may also develop a red swollen area at the site of the injection. There is no need to worry about the symptoms described above as they are completely normal. However, if your baby's temperature rises above 38°C (100.4°F), you must always seek medical advice. If you think your baby is having an adverse reaction to the vaccine, consult your doctor at once, as there is a rare possibility of anaphylaxis (a severe allergic response) with the use of any vaccine.

Development

Mental development

Your baby is now familiar with his surroundings and, during the longer periods when he is awake, he will be beginning to show an interest in objects and an increasing wish to interact with those around him.

- During this second month you may begin to be rewarded with your baby's first smiles. The more eye contact you have with your baby, while responding to his sounds and talking with him, the more likely this is to happen. He may smile at all faces but the biggest smiles are usually kept for those people he knows best.

- He will recognise you and may demonstrate this with his body language. Some babies go rigid or wriggle with excitement when they see those they recognise.

- Some babies are beginning to gurgle with pleasure and squeal with delight. If your baby does this, he will enjoy it if you imitate any new noises he makes, in a pretend 'conversation'. Do not feel embarrassed or self-conscious about talking to your baby in this way.

Physical development

- Your baby's vision has improved and he should now be able to focus clearly on your face. If you move your head slowly, your baby should be able to follow you around with his eyes. He can focus on a brightly coloured toy or object and will also be able to track it with his eyes if it is moved.

- Your baby's hearing is becoming more acute. Not only can he recognise your voice and the voice of his father, he is also beginning to recognise the regular sounds in his life. He might know the dog barking, the radio or the sound of his brothers and sisters playing.

- The 'Moro' reflex and 'grasp' reflex with which he was born are now

Seeing your baby smile for the first time is a wonderful moment

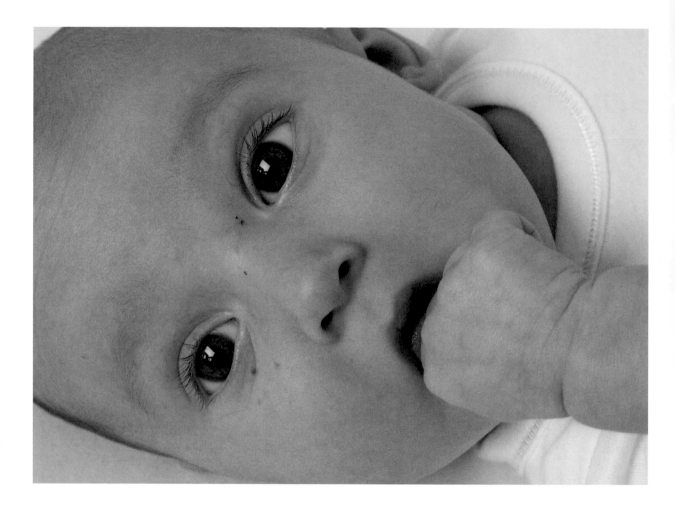

beginning to lessen. He will begin to use his hands to express himself, squeezing them closed when he is crying. His hands are open a lot of the time and he is learning to put his fingers in his mouth. He may try to put his fingers in his mouth to suck them if he is hungry even though he has not yet gained proper control of them.

- Although it will be difficult for him to grasp objects effectively, if you allow your baby to grasp your hand, you might feel him trying to take a little of its weight if you pull away.

- It is not unusual for a baby of this age to be able to hold on to an object, and to try to raise it to his mouth. Do be vigilant regarding what your baby might be able to reach. He is able to focus on small objects, and these need to be kept out of his way in the event that he could put them in his mouth and choke.

- The muscles in your baby's neck are considerably stronger than at birth. He will still need to be supported and handled appropriately, however he can now hold his head upright at times, and should be able to raise his head by 45 degrees when placed for a short period on his tummy.

- The muscles in his legs are developing and some babies will adore being held upright, enjoying straightening their legs to allow them to 'stand' for short periods of time. Your baby will also enjoying kicking with his legs.

Encouraging development through play – four to six weeks

Most babies are much more alert at this age, and will enjoy focusing for longer periods on posters, cards or colourful friezes. Buy a selection of these and stick them to cardboard so they can be moved to different places. Your baby should be showing more interest in his toys, and may be happy to kick under his playgym or mobile for as much as 15–20 minutes (though some babies will get bored before then while others may be happy playing for as much as 30 minutes). He should have more head control now, so encourage him to practise push-ups when he is lying on his tummy on his changing mat (but never leave him alone on the changing mat).

- When you are changing and bathing your baby, allow him to have some supervised 'play' time without a nappy on. Babies love the sensation of being able to extend their legs unimpeded by a nappy and will kick vigorously on a changing mat. Not only does this entertain your baby, it helps to strengthen the muscles in his legs and will also help prevent nappy rash (see page 20).

> **BABY'S TASTES**
> If you are breastfeeding your baby, he might show a preference to the flavour of your milk. For instance, if you have eaten something hot or spicy, this will affect the taste of your breast milk, and your baby might show a lack of enthusiasm. By the end of the second month, your baby's understanding of his new world is nothing short of miraculous. He has learnt to recognise faces, noises and smells. His increasing curiosity regarding his surroundings is becoming more noticeable as he begins to be able to explore by touch and by putting fingers in his mouth.

HEARING TEST
It is not unusual for a GP or nurse to test the hearing of your baby between 6 and 8 weeks. This will be a relatively simple test to establish that your baby responds to sounds. If there is any doubt, your baby will be referred to a consultant for a more scientific procedure.

- Start to show your baby simple baby books for 5-10 minutes each day and point to and name different images. Sing nursery rhymes to him, especially ones with lots of 'S' sounds in them; the shape your mouth makes when singing these songs will encourage him to smile.

Encouraging development through play – six to eight weeks

Your baby should be more alert at all his wakeful times now.

- Continue to let your baby play for short spells alone while you remain within sight of him without interacting. He should be able to do this for at least 15–20 minutes by the end of the month.

- You may have noticed that when your baby lies on his back, his head is often turned to the same side. To encourage him to lie with his head turned both ways, place a brightly coloured toy or book on the other side and draw his attention to it. This will encourage him to lie both ways comfortably.

- Once you have had your six-week check-up you could start taking him to mother-and-baby exercise classes. There are many of these to choose from. Some will focus more on you, while others such as baby yoga will be primarily directed at your baby, but may include some gentle exercises for you as well.

- Baby massage classes can be found which will take babies from around six weeks old, although some may begin at eight to 12 weeks. Provided your baby will remain happily awake for the class length, you will both enjoy the benefits which massage can bring.

Toys, games and books

Your baby will start to show a greater interest in his playgym and musical mobile and he will also enjoy rattles. Other toys he may now like to watch are simple pop-up puppets on sticks. The animal, such as a frog or rabbit, remains

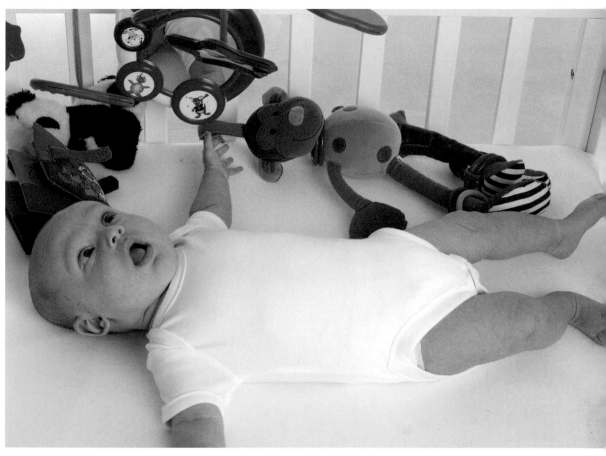

Your baby will now enjoy focusing on more brightly coloured toys

hidden in the cone until the stick is pulled and it suddenly appears.

There are plenty of soft books that have different textures and noises for your baby to enjoy. Also look at some of the board and paperback books aimed at babies slightly older than yours. Provided the pictures are simple and colourful he will enjoy looking at them with you. Borrow some very young picture books from the library and start to read him stories. It doesn't matter if your baby does not understand everything as he will enjoy the sound of your voice and the closeness of sitting with you.

> **TOP TIP**
> 'Tummy time' should now be an established part of your day. Your baby will be happier to spend longer in this position, both on his changing mat and on the floor and his increased head control means that he will begin to take some weight on to his forearms.

Using his hands

By the end of the second month your baby will have become much more aware of his hands and fingers and there are several ways in which you can encourage this new interest:

- Play finger games such as 'This Little Piggy' with him.

- Encourage him to begin to grasp small soft toys, especially textured ones. You can find animals such as toy spiders with different materials used for each leg. Soft bricks can also be found with each side made from a different fabric. Make your baby aware of these by stroking them across his palms and the backs of his hands, telling him 'This is soft' , 'This is fluffy', as you let him experience the different textures.

- By the end of two months your baby should be able to briefly hold on to a small rattle when put into his hand. His grasp reflex is beginning to disappear but he will be able to hold on for a short while. The best rattles to use are the small soft ones that have a ring topped with the head of a teddy or other animal. The ring needs to be small enough for your baby to get his palm around it. Small, light plastic ring-type rattles can also be good for a baby of this age.

- Spending time under his playgym will encourage your baby to start batting at the toys hanging down. From around six weeks he may get an occasional hit, but his movements will still be quite uncoordinated.

Music and sounds

Your baby may now have favourite songs that you sing, and he may be calmed by certain pieces of music.

- Continue to encourage his hearing by getting him to listen to wind chimes, ticking clocks, bells and even sounds such as the wind in the trees. Drawing his attention to different sounds and noises will help widen his experience of the world and make him more aware.

● You may like to have a radio or some music playing in the background during the day, especially if you are on your own with the baby but do try to have quiet times when you switch them off. Encourage your baby to hold longer 'conversations' with you now he can make sounds. You will be more aware of the sounds that he is trying to make if there is no noise in the background.

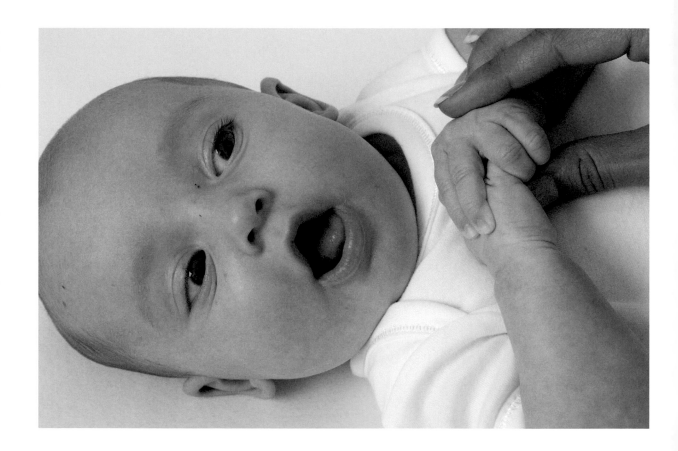

Encourage your baby to hold longer 'conversations' with you now he can make sounds

Q&A

swaddling

Q

My daughter, who is just seven weeks, has always slept well with no sleep association problems. The problem is that she loves being swaddled but just recently she has been waking more during the night (and sometimes between 7 and 10pm) and appears to be fighting to get out of the swaddle. I have tried to take the swaddle away, but she flails her arms around and won't settle unless I rock her (which I don't want to do long term as it may cause a sleep association problem).

A

Now that your daughter is almost two months old it is important to get her used to sleeping unswaddled so as to prevent the dangers that may occur through overheating.

As she still thrashes about when sleeping, use the following method to get her used to being half-swaddled, before removing the swaddle completely. Start with the nap she has at 8.45am and swaddle her as usual, but leave one arm free. If you can, remember to alternate the arm which is left out each morning. As this is a short nap she should not be too disturbed. After a few days of this, begin to do the same thing at 7pm

as well, while continuing to swaddle her fully for the night after her 10.30pm feed. After a few days, once she is used to one arm being left out at the shorter naps, use the same method of swaddling through the night, leaving alternate arms free. You will gradually be able to half-swaddle her with both arms free (see page 00) (This now relates to the half-swaddling info on p. 58, which I have queried.

Q

Up to the age of six weeks my son was only waking once in the night, usually between 2 and 3am, feeding well and settling back to sleep until nearer 7am. For the last 10 days he has been waking up twice a night, usually around 2am then again at 5am.

A

Babies go through a growth spurt at six weeks and it is possible that this is what has triggered the twice-a-night waking. I would suggest that you try giving a split feed at the late feed until this problem is resolved and he is back to waking up once in the night again. By having him awake longer and giving him a slightly bigger feed he should soon begin to sleep one longer

stretch in the night again.

For the late-evening split feed to be effective, it is important to begin to wake your baby by 9.45pm and make sure he is fully awake before feeding him. Turn on the lights brightly and remove any covers from him. Babies can be sleepy at this time of the day so you may need to undo his sleep suit and expose his legs to the air to fully wake him. Offer him the first breast or as much as he will take from the bottle. Then allow him to spend some time kicking on his play mat, but do not overstimulate him too much by talking a lot at this time. Keep a close eye on him for signs of tiredness. Between 10.45 and 11pm, you should take him to the bedroom, change his nappy, dim the lights and offer the second breast. If you are bottle-feeding he should be offered a small top-up feed of freshly heated milk, do not reheat any left-over milk from his earlier feed. Ensure he is well winded and settled back in his cot by 11.15pm, making sure that he is well tucked in, and that the sheet and blanket go under the mattress enough that he can not kick his covers off in the night, which is another reason that babies often start to wake up earlier in the night.

The
Third
Month

D URING THE FIRST COUPLE OF MONTHS IT IS OFTEN HARD TO DEFINE
your baby's needs but during the third month he will be able to
express his needs much more, both physically and emotionally. He
will start to develop his own little character, using his body movements to
demonstrate his feelings of happiness, anger, boredom, tiredness, etc. He will be
responding to you with lots of smiles and gurgles as you talk to him. He will also
recognise familiar faces and enjoy going on regular outings to the same places,
such as the local park or baby group.

Outings with babies need not always be to places that are specifically
baby-orientated. I used to find that my babies loved looking around the art galleries, shopping centres and museums that I took them to, so it is always worth
trying new places, even ones that seem geared towards adults. Trips out can be
interesting for you as well!

As your baby is beginning to develop more muscle control, you can now get
him involved with various different activities, such as baby swimming classes and
baby gym. Remember the whole aim of these activities is for you and your baby
to have fun and enjoy yourselves. You will see lots of other babies at these events
so bear in mind that all babies develop at a different rate and try not to get
worried if your baby is not yet doing what some of the other babies are doing.

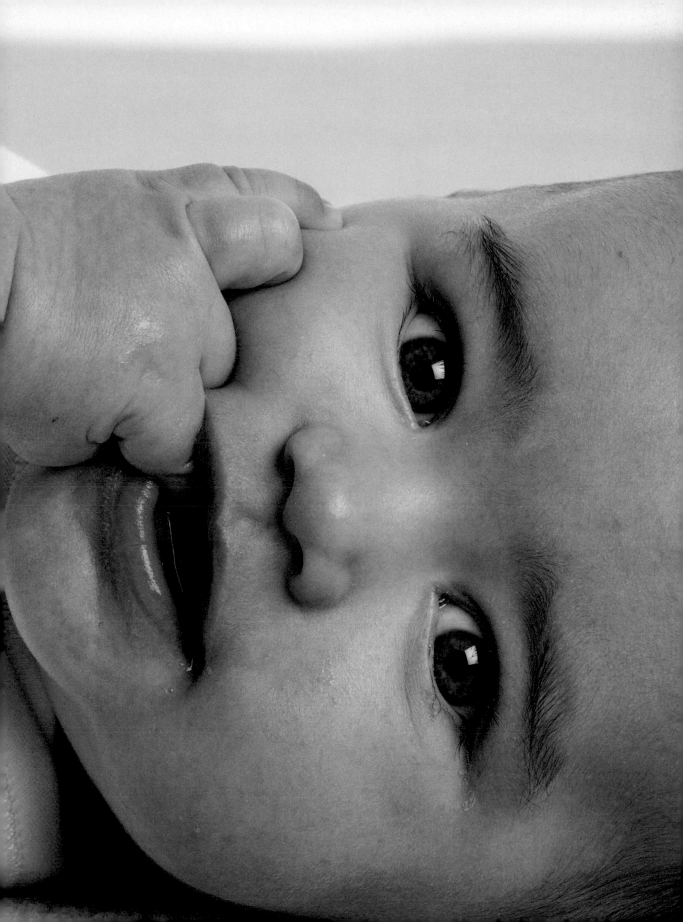

Feeding

- If you have been following a routine, your baby's feed times should be more established during the day, and he should be managing to sleep a longer spell from his last feed at 10.30pm.

- The lengths of times of feeds may be much shorter now, and many babies can take a full breast-feed in 15–20 minutes or even less.

- Be guided by your baby as to how long he needs on the breast. If he is managing to go between three and four hours during daytime feeds, and if your health visitor is happy with his weight gain, he is obviously getting enough milk, so do not worry about the length of feeds.

Feeding at night

- Some babies of this age can manage to get right through to 7am from the late feed, while others may still be waking up around 5am needing a quick feed to get them back to sleep until 7am.

- If your baby is still waking up and needing to be fed at around 2–3am in the night, it is very possible that he is not getting enough during the day, or at the last feed.

- Sometimes, changing the feed at 10.30pm to a split feed at 10pm and 11.15pm, and keeping him awake during this time will help him sleep a longer spell in the night.

- Try keeping a feeding and sleeping diary for a week to see whether there is any other reason why he is not going longer in the night.

Try to increase his daytime milk during growth spurts so that he does not regress on his night-time feeding.

The nine-week growth spurt

- Your baby is likely to go through a further growth spurt at around nine weeks of age and he will look for extra milk during this stage.

- Try to increase his daytime milk during growth spurts so that he does not regress on his night-time feeding.

- During growth spurts your baby may need to go back to feeding for longer on the breast for a few days and be offered top-up feeds before naps.

- If you are expressing milk this may help during growth spurts (see page 36).

Sleeping

During the third month your baby should manage to stay awake more easily for longer periods. However, because he is also becoming much more physically active, it is important to watch that he does not become overtired. He will still probably need to sleep within a couple of hours of waking up, so try to stick to regular naptimes during the day as much as possible. If he is to sleep well at night-time, his daytime sleep should not add up to much more than three and a half hours in total between the hours of 7am and 7pm, reducing to three hours by the end of three months. This should be divided up into three separate naps and your baby should now be half-swaddled when he goes down for all of his sleeps.

If your baby is having a short nap in the morning, and a good nap of two hours or more at lunchtime, he may only need a very short nap in the late afternoon. However, if he has only had a short nap at lunchtime he will need to have a slightly longer nap in the afternoon if he is not to get overtired at bedtime. Remember that he should not sleep any later than 5pm if you want him to be ready for his night-time sleep at 7pm.

> **RESTLESS NIGHTS**
> You may find that your more active baby is now waking in the night because he is getting out of his half-swaddle and moving around the cot. If this is happening, it is a good idea to get him a lightweight sleeping bag. Because a baby of this age still has a fairly strong 'Moro' reflex, choosing the lightest tog of 0.5 will mean that you can still use a thin cotton sheet across the top of him to make him feel secure, without the risk of overheating.

The bed and bathtime routine

Continue with the established bathtime routine and ensure your baby has his bath at 5.45pm each day and that he is massaged and dressed and ready for a feed at 6.15pm. Around this time your baby may not be so sleepy when you finish his feed. If this is the case, you can lay him in his cot with the lights dimmed, and with a little book or toy to look at for a short spell.

As he starts to drift off, you should then give him a kiss and say goodnight. Remove the book and switch off the light so he is aware that you are leaving the room, and that it is time to go to sleep.

Immunisation

 AFTER-EFFECTS OF VACCINATIONS

Your baby may react to the MenC vaccination with a mild temperature, irritability, headache and/or redness or swelling at the site of the injection. Research has shown that approximately half of the babies who have been immunised will become irritable, while one in 20 will get a mild fever. However, as before, if your baby's temperature rises above 38°C (100.4°F), or if you think your child has had an adverse reaction to the vaccine, you must always seek medical advice immediately.

At the age of three months your baby will be given a second DTaP/IPV/Hib immunisation to boost his immunity against diphtheria, tetanus, pertussis (whooping cough), polio and haemophilus influenzae type b (Hib).

Your baby will now be offered his first dose of MenC vaccine, an immunisation that offers protection against meningococcal group C infection. This infection can cause meningitis and septicaemia. The vaccine does not provide protection against meningitis caused by bacteria other than the meningococcal group C type or by viruses.

A second MenC immunisation will be given at four months and a dose of combined Hib/MenC vaccine is also given at twelve months.

For more information and advice on concerns about vaccinations, see page 73.

Development

Mental development

During the third month, your baby will be becoming increasingly vocal. Not only may he be able to coo, blow raspberries and gurgle, he may also squeal with pleasure, bellow with annoyance and laugh with joy. The more you can encourage these noises, the better. Exaggerate your responses. Look at him when you talk to enable him to see your mouth. Smile with pleasure when he makes new noises. Enjoy experimenting with sound when you are playing with him.

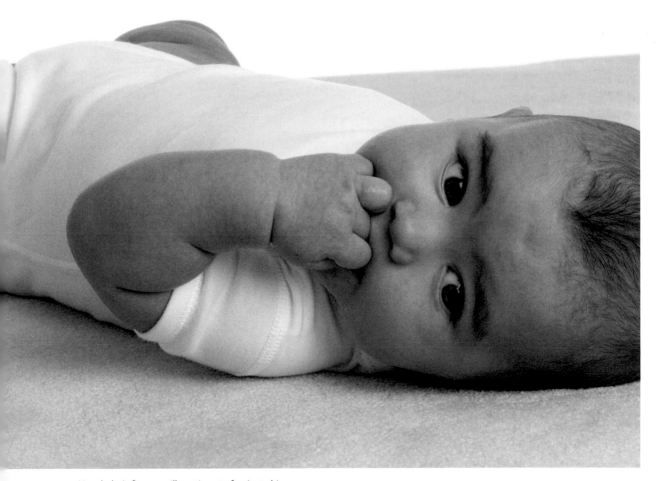

Your baby's fingers will continue to fascinate him

If you have made
the decision to use
a dummy, this is a
good month to
consider reducing
its usage

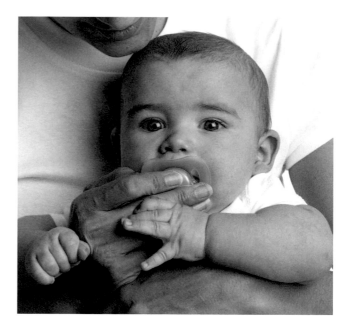

- He will start to respond to familiar noises with a noticeable reaction. Loud noises will startle him and some noises will cause amusement. Singing and music will stimulate and soothe him.

- Your baby can now anticipate certain parts of his day. He will associate the sound of running water with having a bath and may get excited at the sound. He may reach out when he sees his bottle near by and begin to try to place his hands around it. Where possible, your baby will be using 'mouthing' to explore the world around him. He will be putting his fingers in his mouth, and sucking on anything within his reach. Sometimes a baby of this age will lick his lips when he sees his mother's nipple or his milk bottle.

- If you have made the decision to use a dummy or comforter to settle your baby, this is a good time to consider reducing its usage. Babies of twelve weeks are adaptable, and now that your baby is in a routine, he will soon adjust to the removal of his soother. His cognitive powers are such that if you continue giving him a soother he will become increasingly dependent on it, and a habit may form.

- Your baby will continue to be intrigued by his fingers and he will begin to connect his thoughts of opening and closing his hands to making the actual movements. He should be able to link his fingers, and to put them in his mouth.

- It is not unusual for your baby to smile when he hears your voice. The first smiles your baby gave you were a combination of reflex and pleasure. By the third month, you can be in no doubt that his smiles are ones of delight in seeing you, or something that has pleased him. Some babies may even manage a gurgly laugh.

- There is nothing your baby likes more than company.

Physical development

By the end of the third month you will notice that your baby is far more co-ordinated in his movements. He will enjoy kicking vigorously and using his arms and hands. By the end of this month he should be able to grasp hold of a hanging toy on his baby gym. His swiping and batting will be better aimed as his hand–to–eye coordination improves.

- Your baby should be able to turn his head to enable himself to watch a moving object 15–20 cm away. His neck muscles have strengthened to allow him to look around. He should be able to stay awake easily when he is out in the buggy, and will enjoy sitting slightly elevated so that he can look around.

- He is becoming much stronger in his upper body and should be able to hold his head up for a few minutes while he is lying on his tummy.

- When placed on his back, your baby will enjoy kicking his legs, particularly when you let him lie on his changing mat without a nappy. He can kick his legs alternately or in tandem.

Your baby should be able to hold his head up now that his upper body is stonger

91

He will enjoy pushing up on his arms – encourage this by holding things up for him to look at

Encouraging development through play – eight to twelve weeks

Your baby is beginning to gain control of his own body and is developing the strength in his limbs to be able to move around with greater ease.

- Encourage your baby to reach out for his toys by holding them above him so that he can reach up and grasp them. His grasp reflex is fast disappearing and he will now need to learn how to hold on to objects before he can play with rattles and other toys.

- Play lots of exercise games with your baby that involve his legs and arms, cycling and moving his arms and legs alternately. Encourage him to roll from his back on to his front (see page 109 for more on helping encourage him to roll).

Encourage him to roll from his back on to his front by playing games that involve his arms and legs

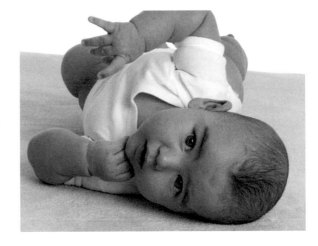

- Your baby will play with his fingers, lacing them together and often bringing both hands up in front of his face, especially when lying on his back. This 'handregard' is a developmental stage. Soon he will be using both hands to hold and manipulate toys and other objects. He may pull and pluck at his clothes and blankets.

- When vocalising his whole body will be involved, with lots of kicking and waving of his arms. He will now probably enjoy meeting other babies at a mother and baby group; both children of his own age and those slightly older will fascinate him.

- Having spent time each day on his tummy for the last three months your baby should now be happy to stay in this position for longer periods. He will enjoy pushing up on his arms as he gradually gains control and strength in his upper body. Placing a baby mirror in front of him that can be propped at an angle, or one that is wedge-shaped, will encourage him to really push up to catch sight of his reflection. Lying down beside your baby can also be reassuring for him.

Toys, games and books

Rattles are an ideal toy for this age group and there are many types around. Have a really good look at the different types before you buy one. Your baby will be spending a good deal of his playtime lying on the floor and holding things above his face. As his coordination is not yet that well developed he will often bring his hands close to his face. If he is holding a hard or heavy rattle this may result in a nasty knock and a big surprise to him, probably causing him to cry from the shock. While accidents such as these are bound to occur from time to time, try to minimise them by finding light, soft or easily held rattles and toys.

BATH TOYS

Your baby will start to take an interest in bath toys. Plastic ducks always fascinate, especially those contained within a clear plastic ball along with coloured pieces of plastic suspended in liquid. There are plenty of bath toys around but many will not really be suitable until your baby is able to sit alone in the bath, without your support. Find one or two of the simple squirting types of plastic animals and watch his face when you squirt a stream of water from a height on to his tummy. He may reach out and try to grasp it, and be amazed that the water just trickles over his hands.

- Many of the small toys which are found hanging from mobiles, gyms, activity arches and cot bars are suitable for your baby to try to hold. Their colours will attract him and they will have textures and noises to further gain his attention.

- There are some very simple wooden rattles and toys around that will be a good contrast to his soft ones. The cage-type rattle containing a bell can easily be held. He will also enjoy holding the simple rings with beads threaded on to spindles to be shaken, giving him a different sound to listen to. Remember that, eventually, everything will go into his mouth so make sure you buy rattles and toys that carry the safety standard symbol.

- He will enjoy exploring 'feely' books while sitting on your lap. There are many to choose from, some soft, others of the board variety. Show him how to turn the pages, which will be easier when they are made of stiff card. Point to the pictures and tell him what they are. Make appropriate sounds if you like and begin to make time every day to enjoy a few books together.

TOP TIP
It's a good idea to go swimming once a week and to attend one other social activity, such as a playgroup.

He will want to put rattles in his mouth so make sure you buy toys that carry the safety standard symbol

Encouraging develoment through play – twelve to fourteen weeks

Towards the end of three months, your baby should be quite active during his social hours, spending plenty of time on the floor kicking and rolling, reaching for toys and holding them for short spells. Encourage lots of grabbing and holding.

- He should still be having 'tummy time' for a short spell every day.

- Continue reading to your baby every day and make sure he listens to a wide variety of music.

- Encourage him to grasp his own bottle, but never allow him to feed by himself or prop the bottle up.

Q&A

nap time

Q

My husband is away on business for some time, so I have taken our nine-week-old baby to stay with my parents. Anna is used to a very quiet environment, as our home is in the countryside and it is also sound-proofed. If I knew there was going to be a noise outside I would switch on some 'white noise' in her room so her sleep was not disturbed. Now we are staying with my parents who live on a road with cars and lorries frequently going past. There are so many adults staying in the house that it is impossible for the house to be quiet all the time. Anna is sleeping well at night, as once into a deep sleep the noise doesn't disturb her. However, it is proving impossible for her to get enough sleep by day, as it is either too noisy for her to settle, or a sudden noise will wake her up. My wonderful contented baby has become an overtired, crying baby.

A

In time, Anna will probably adjust to the noise level outside the house. But it will then be time for you to return home and she will have to adjust to the quiet again.

If you could set up a CD player in her room by day, try using some gentle, natural sounds to mask out the other noises that are disturbing her. This would be especially useful to block out the sound of traffic outside. Put the CD on at a moderate level before she goes down for a nap. If this is not possible, try tuning a radio in between stations to get the 'white noise' sound. This could help her, as it did in the past when you were home.

Ask the other members of the household to respect Anna's need for sleep and, although they do not have to remain totally silent, at least ask them to try to not make any sudden noises during her nap times. Doors being banged shut are always preventable, as are loud voices near to her room. If you explain to them that Anna will be a far happier baby when awake if she does sleep well, it might be possible to get her to settle better. Many adults think that a baby can sleep through anything. This is often true in the early weeks once they are asleep, but as they mature they need more peaceful conditions Depending where her room is situated in the house, sudden, loud noises such as dishwashers being

emptied or pans being washed will be enough to wake her. Is there another room she could use by day to sleep in which is in a quieter part of the house?

Try to take her for a walk in her pram every other day or so, especially over the long lunchtime nap. This will not be enough to make Anna begin to associate sleep with the movement of a pram, but it would help her catch up a little. Some mothers who do take their babies out at the lunchtime nap find that draping a blanket over the pram or buggy helps their baby sleep well. Using times out and away from the noise of the house and the road would be beneficial to you both, as it is very easy to become tense in a situation such as this and Anna could well pick up on your tensions and become unsettled herself.

Q

My 11-week-old baby has just become established in a regular routine of feeding and sleeping. However, we have recently been invited to visit my parents, who live a long distance away, so we will need to stay several days to make the trip worthwhile. I am worried

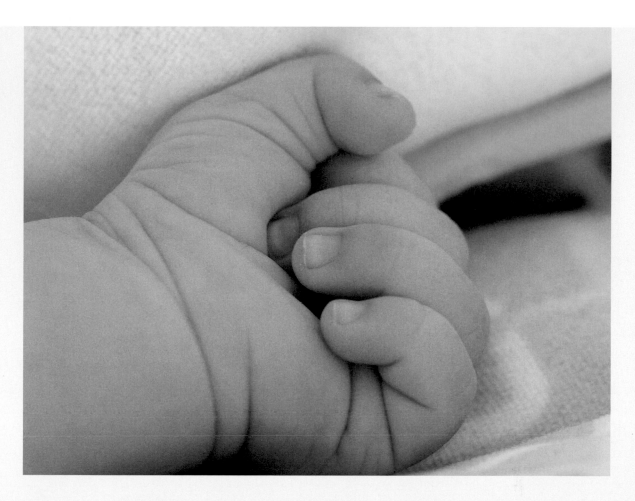

that his routines will be broken during the stay and that all my hard work will be wasted. Do you have any advice?

As you are about to stay with grandparents who do not see their grandchild on a regular basis, remember that they will be very excited about the visit. Their priority will probably be to spend as much time as possible cuddling and playing with the baby so they may not understand your concern to try and keep him in the routine that you have established. Try, if possible, to let them have a run-down of his sleeping and waking times before you go to stay. Explain what you have been doing, letting them know how happy their grand-child is now that he is in a pattern of regular sleep/feed times. Put lots of emphasis on your baby spending 'special time' with Granny and Grandpa when he is awake, rather than emphasising that they can't play with him at certain times because he is supposed to be asleep.

Take the opportunity, should they offer to baby-sit, for you and your partner to have a nice lunch or dinner out. It is possible you will get back to a baby whose sleep has been disrupted, but try not to get too uptight about it. It is more important that you help to develop a really good relationship between your baby and his grandparents than get annoyed with them because they woke him an hour earlier than usual.

The Fourth Month

AT THIS AGE YOUR BABY WILL REALLY START TO ENJOY GAMES AND activities that are repetitive and which include lots of songs and actions. If you have not already done so, this is a great time to take part in a couple of organised play dates or events where lots of other babies are joining in with musical rhymes. Babies of this age particularly like toddlers and small children, so do not feel that you should always mix with mothers who have a baby the same age as yours.

During your baby's fourth month his eye and hand coordination is developing rapidly and he will start to grasp at everything within reach that is of interest to him. Be warned – earrings, necklaces and spectacles will all be objects of great fascination and it will be of no concern to him that your ear lobe is attached to the earring he is tugging at! Divert his attention from these attractions by encouraging him to play with his own toys; he may now begin to amuse himself with these, making babbling and cooing noises as he does so.

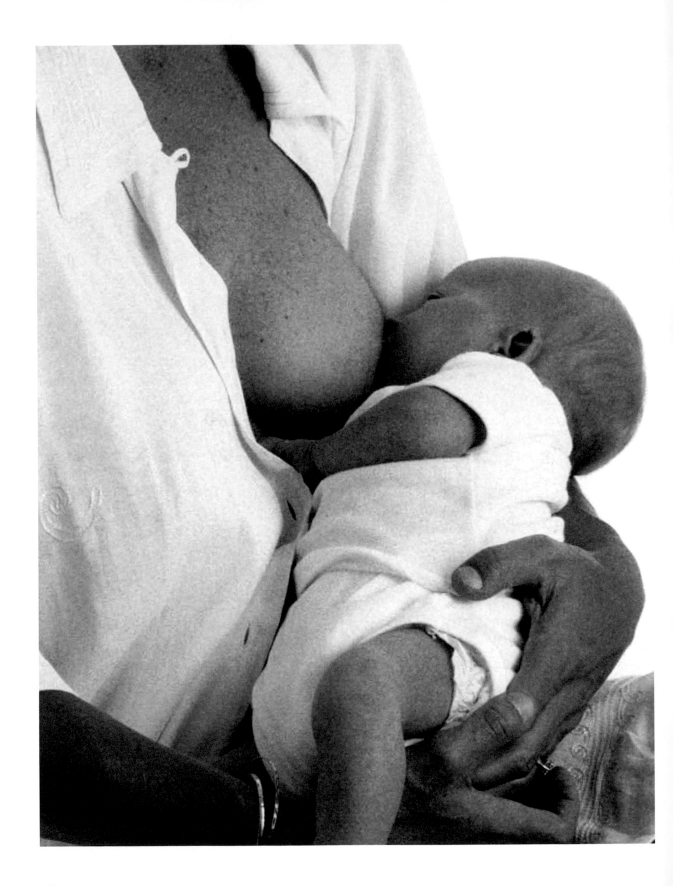

Getting used to other carers

If you are planning to go back to work when your baby is between six and nine months old, it is a good idea to start getting him used to being left with someone else on a regular basis, once or twice a week.

- Start off by leaving him for half an hour at a time, gradually building it up to two or three hours. The more you are able to do this, the easier it will be to leave your baby for a longer period when you finally go back to work.

- You will also need to be researching local child-care provision in preparation for going back to work, which may involve interviewing nannies or child-minders, looking around nursery schools and working out the family finances.

- Even if you are not planning on going back to work, finding someone you trust and who can look after your baby on a regular basis, is still just as important.

Feeding

Your baby should hopefully be well established on five milk feeds a day now, and sleeping through until nearer 6/7am in the morning from his 10.30pm feed at night.

- If you find that he suddenly starts to wake up early or in the middle of the night again, and refuses to settle back to sleep quickly, it would be best to assume that he is going through a growth spurt and needs extra milk.

- Because parents are now advised to wait until six months before introducing solids, some

> **TOP TIP**
> Don't use time away from your baby to do domestic chores. Take the opportunity for a little 'me' time. It is so important for a mother's morale to have some time away by herself. A little pampering or simply a break for a coffee and reading a magazine can feel like a holiday after the intensity of the first months of motherhood.

PLANNING YOUR RETURN TO WORK

If you are returning to work when your baby is between six and nine months old and he is exclusively breastfed, it is a good idea to start thinking about introducing a bottle of expressed milk or formula at one of his day feeds, if you have not already done the former, to get him used to taking a bottle.

If you are unable to express milk and you have decided to switch to formula, it is important to plan the transition from breastfeeding to bottle-feeding properly. When deciding for how long you intend to breast-feed your baby, you should take into consideration that once you have established a good milk supply, you must allow approximately a week to drop each breastfeed. For example, it can take six weeks to establish a good milk supply and if you decide to give up breastfeeding, you should allow, at the very least, a further five weeks to drop all breastfeeds and to establish bottle-feeding. If you give up breastfeeding before you have established a good milk supply you should still allow enough time for your baby to get used to feeding from the bottle. Some babies can get very upset if they suddenly lose the pleasure and comfort they get from breastfeeding.

For a mother who has breastfed for less than a month, I generally advise a period of 3–4 days in between dropping feeds. For a mother who has been breastfeeding longer than a month, it is best to allow 5–7 days in between dropping feeds. The best way to do this is gradually to reduce the length of time the baby feeds from the breast by five minutes each day and top up with formula. Once your baby is taking a full bottle-feed, the breastfeed can be dropped. If you plan the weaning carefully and gradually, your baby will have time to adjust to the bottle and you will avoid the risk of developing mastitis, which can happen when a feed is instantly dropped and the milk ducts become blocked due to engorgement.

babies who have slept through for several weeks will often need to have a sixth feed re-introduced to satisfy their hunger.

- If you find that re-introducing a middle-of-the-night feed does not appear to be satisfying your baby's increased hunger, then you should discuss this with your health visitor. While six months is the recommended age for introducing solids, all babies are different and it may be that you will be advised to introduce solids slightly earlier than six months.

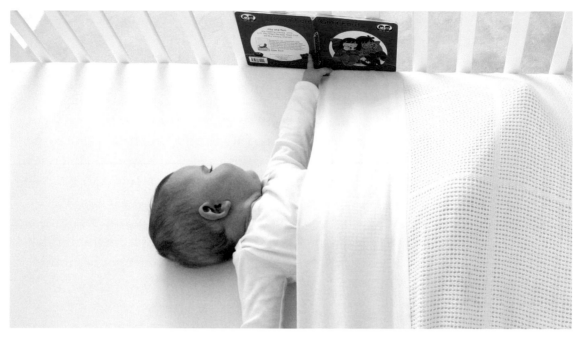

Tuck your baby's sheet in firmly so that she can't roll on to her tummy. Make sure any books or toys are also tucked in very firmly so that she can't grasp them and hurt herself. Remove them during sleep times.

Sleeping

- Provided your baby's nutritional needs are being met, he should manage to sleep well between 7pm and 6–7am, with a very quick and sleepy late feed although some larger breastfed babies may continue to wake at 5am needing a short feed.

- Babies of four to five months of age need a maximum of three hours sleep between the hours of 7am and 7pm. This should be divided up into two or three separate naps.

- It is important that your baby is still put to sleep on his back at this stage, and to avoid him rolling over on to his tummy you should still tuck him in firmly with a thin cotton sheet.

- If he is sleeping well during his morning naps, your baby may now be able to go through the afternoon without a further nap. However, on days that you take him out for lunch, you will probably find that he does not sleep the full two hours and will need a short nap of 20–40 minutes between 4pm and 5pm, if he is not to get overtired at bedtime.

Sleeping bags

Many babies start to push their way up to the top of the cot at this age. They get out of their half-swaddle and covers, find themselves stuck in the corner and they become distressed. Putting them in a sleeping bag will help prevent this. However, if your baby still has a very strong 'Moro reflex and is thrashing his legs a lot in the night, you may still need to make him feel more secure by putting a thin cotton sheet across the top of him, making sure it is well tucked in under the mattress. When doing this it is important that you only use a 0.5 sleeping bag to ensure that your baby does not become overheated.

The bed and bathtime routine

> **BATHTIME SAFETY**
> Your baby may now be in the big bath and it is ever more important to be vigilant during bathtime. You will need to use a rubber bath mat on the bottom of the bath to prevent slipping and you must always supervise your baby as young children can quickly drown in very shallow water. Always make sure you have everything you need to hand before bathing your baby and never leave him unattended.

Continue with the established bathtime routine and ensure your baby has his bath at 5.45pm each day and that he is massaged and dressed and ready for a feed at 6.15pm.

Bathtime fun

Bathtime will now be an enjoyable part of your baby's day. He knows what to expect and may get very excited when put in the water. He should be able to pat the water now and may cause some hefty splashes! Provided he doesn't mind having water on his face he will carry on with this fun, so don't rush to dry him off. Once he is able to hold his head steady, he may prefer to sit up in the bath, as long as you support him well. He will then be able to watch his toys and enjoy the sensations of splashing.

Immunisation

At four months of age your baby will be given further immunisations for DTaP/IPV/Hib, MenC and PCV. These follow on from the vaccinations he received at two and three months and his immunity will be further boosted. The gaps between the different doses of vaccines are there to ensure that each dose has time to work.

See page 88 for details of possible after-effects.

Development

Mental development

Your baby is awake for considerably longer periods of time by four to five months and his ability to concentrate is growing. He will be visually stimulated by everything around him. Now that he is so much more aware of all that is going on you may find he needs to take his feeds in a quiet room where he will not be distracted.

- It is not unusual for a baby of this age to be more suspicious of people he doesn't know, while responding with greater enthusiasm to his loved ones. He will still smile at most people but may be happier to smile at them from the safety of your arms.

- He will love looking at himself in a mirror, and will be curious to see the reflections of his loved ones.

> Your baby will be visually stimulated by everything around him

- Your baby's hearing is now sharp enough for him to be able to recognise where the sound comes from. He is increasingly responsive to music and chatter and is associating sounds with various activities. He will recognise his parent's voices and those of his brothers and sisters.

Your baby may be happier to greet other people when you're holding her so she feels safe

- Your baby will anticipate his feeds from the breast or the bottle in a physical manner. Some babies begin to squeal with delight or even cry when they see their bottle, such is their eagerness to be fed.

- He will continue to show his pleasure with more frequent chuckles and laughter. It may be something specific which causes your baby to laugh – a noise that you make or a toy which particularly appeals to him. It might also take a week or two for him to repeat his laughter, and then gradually this will become a more regular response.

Physical development

Your baby is fast learning to coordinate his sight with his hand movements. Every day he will be picking up toys and other items with greater dexterity. Since he can now control and direct his hands he might be becoming a thumb-sucker. If so, there is no need to worry, as most children grow out of this habit naturally.

- By four months of age, the development of the neck muscles enables your baby to support his head steadily. He may well show a greater wish to be sitting up rather than playing on his tummy or back. Most babies of this age need to be well supported when sitting, though very occasionally a baby of four to five months can sit up without support. Those babies who are not able to sit usually enjoy being propped up since it gives them the best view of their surroundings. Never leave your baby on his own, unsupervised. Even the relative safety of a specially designed baby play ring will not stop a four-month-old from slipping or wriggling into a less secure position.

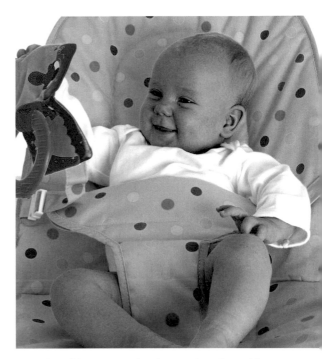
Your baby will love sitting in her chair watching the world

- Your baby will continually surprise you by doing things that you weren't aware he could do. He will be reaching further, picking up objects and moving into positions that compromise his safety.

- Your baby might be able to roll over in one direction when playing on his back or lying in his cot. Never leave your baby unattended on a changing station or bed, since if he rolls over while you are momentarily out of the room, he might hurt himself.

- When lying on his tummy, your baby should be able to lift his head by 90 degrees. He will also be able to use his forearms to raise himself up a little.

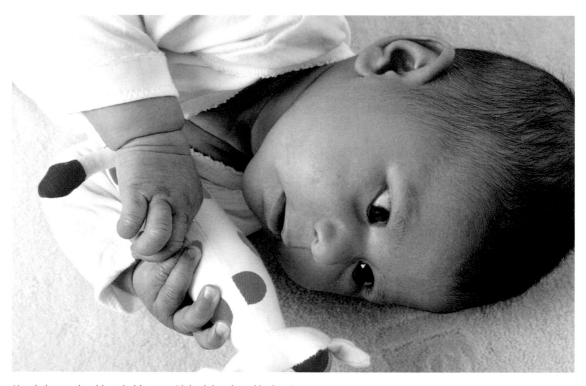

Your baby may be able to hold a toy with both hands and look at it

Encouraging development through play

Your baby will spend most of his social time on the floor kicking and rolling, reaching for toys and holding them for short spells. Encourage lots of grabbing and holding and help him to hold his own bottle. He should still go on his tummy for a short spell every day and be read to daily. Keep up the swimming and other social activities.

• Once he has been given one of his rattles or toys he will hold it with both hands and look at it for a short while. He then may bring it up to his mouth and begin to suck or chew on it. Your baby's mouth is very sensitive and he will use it as a way of exploring both taste and texture. Be careful when selecting playthings once he begins to 'mouth' his toys since everything he holds is likely to end up in his mouth.

• Your baby can now have a 'conversation' with you, even though he is making only a few discernable sounds. He will answer you back when you speak directly to him. You, in turn, can reply and, once more, he will return with

Your baby's mouth is very sensitive and she will begin to 'mouth' her toys as a means of exploring taste and texture

his answer within a few seconds. Be patient and wait for him when he does start to converse in this way, as he will enjoy the interaction with you.

- As your baby becomes more active when playing on the floor, encourage him. Hold toys to one side of him so that he rolls one way, then move the toy to the other side so that he rolls back.

- Now he is so used to spending time on his tummy he will be able to explore his playmat, which may have flaps and mirrors attached and make different sounds when squeezed or scrunched. He should be able to balance himself on one arm while using the other to explore with. Let him find things for himself rather than always showing him, and watch to see if he can remember where the different activities are when he is put down to play.

TOP TIP
Although your baby should now be happy to play alone for 20–30 minutes at a time (if he has been used to doing so from an early age) he will really enjoy it when you play games with him.

Toys, games and books

This is a lovely time to introduce new games to encourage your baby's development and ability.

- Your baby will adore playing 'Hide and seek' and 'Peekaboo'. Try hiding your face behind your hands or a muslin square, then quickly reappear while saying, 'Peekaboo!'. Hide your face behind a door or sofa, asking 'Where's Mummy?', then pop out to make him laugh. These games will help him learn to understand that although he cannot see your face, you do still exist. He learns to anticipate and uses his memory to recall where you are. He will soon learn how to copy you and will pull a cloth away to reveal your face, causing more laughter.

- Provide him with bought or home-made wrist rattles. These little bands usually have a small soft toy attached to them, sometimes containing a bell

Encourage your baby to roll by putting objects out of her reach

so that they make a sound when he moves his arms. He may also enjoy bug socks. Again, you may like to make your own. Attach a small soft toy tightly to a sock and let your baby try to reach it when he is wearing the socks.

- He will now enjoy more complex toys and rattles that have plenty of bits to occupy his fingers. Look for rings of plastic keys, soft cubes which pull out to reveal squeakers, teethers and mirrors with extra attachments, all of which help develop fine motor skills.

- To help your baby continue to improve his coordination and memory skills, look for toys that provide simple cause and effect. Activity centres where he needs to pull on a string or press a lever to ring a bell or pop up a toy are good for this age, as are simple toys which light up when a certain place is pushed. He will begin to remember what he needs to do from one play session to the next.

- Continue to share books with him as much as you can. He may enjoy the 'feely' ones at certain times in the day, and at others want just to listen to the sound of your voice. Keep a selection of books in various places around the house so you can always have some close by.

- Now that he has more control over the upper half of his body he will like to sit facing you, on your knee, while you hold him by his arms and sing an action rhyme with him. 'Humpty Dumpty' and 'This is the way the ladies ride' will help him learn to anticipate certain actions. He will like being jiggled up and down in time with the words and will probably laugh when you make him fall down between your legs. He may also enjoy 'Round and round the garden' played gently on his palms and may chuckle when tickled under his arms. He will now readily laugh at things that amuse him.

Keep a selection of toys and books in various places around the house so you can always have some close by

Q&A sensitive baby

Q

My 17-week-old daughter is a very grumpy baby and seems to cry more than other children I see. She hates any fuss and screams when getting dressed, having a coat put on and being put into a car seat or a pram. While other babies I see at baby massage class lie there laughing, my daughter disrupts the class with crying and leaves me looking inadequate and embarrassed. She also needs quite constant attention and holding, rocking, singing to and playing with, etc.

Am I doing something wrong or is there something else I could be doing to help? She doesn't seem tired except at night after bathtime and before feeding. She can't be hungry and she sleeps from 6.30pm to 6.30am most nights and loves her food so I have little to complain about. I just want her to be happier.

A

Babies all have different temperaments, in the same way that adults do. Some babies seem to take the world in their stride while others find it quite a bewildering and overwhelming place. If your daughter is a baby who is rather

sensitive she may take longer to get used to new situations, such as a massage class. This doesn't mean you have to stop taking her out and about to meet other babies and children but you may need to help her to get used to the world.

Reassure your daughter by always telling her what is going to happen next. Although it may take longer to get her ready to go out, try talking through the process with her each time. For example, when preparing her for the massage class, tell her that you are going to get her undressed and talk to her reassuringly as you go through the process. During the class keep part of her body covered up with a muslin or small towel as many babies do not like the feel of air on their skin. If she needs to be picked up and cuddled during the session then do so. Gradually, as she feels

more secure, she should begin to enjoy the class. Handling a sensitive baby takes time and patience and it may be a while before she becomes reassured. Until this happens she will prefer not to be moved suddenly from one activity to another.

Comparing your daughter with other babies of her age is not going to help her. All babies develop at a different rate and have different temperaments. Look at your daughter as her own unique character. She may not be so willing to lie and gurgle when massaged but she may be able to lift her head well when on her tummy. Your own attitude is important as well. If you are tense and worried that she may cry when being massaged, she probably will cry. Try to relax and enjoy being with other mums for their company rather than compar-

Try to relax and enjoy being with other mums for their company rather than comparing your baby with theirs

ing your baby with theirs. If you relax, your daughter will begin to do so as well.

It is also a good idea if your daughter becomes more used to amusing herself for short periods of time. Choose a time of day when your daughter is not getting hungry or tired. Keep your own attitude playful and light. Lay out her play-mat with two toys such as a mirror and a book of simple pictures. Talk to her as you lay her down, and then sit beside her. If she starts to

cry straight away, don't pick her up. Talk to her about the pictures in the book or tap on the mirror. If she does begin to take an interest in the book or mirror, quietly observe her rather than talking to her all the time. All babies need plenty of interaction but they also need time on their own to find out things for them-selves. Make the first few occasions short but gradually increase the time she will amuse herself, by looking at or holding a simple toy, without needing your interaction.

There will still be plenty of times when you do need to pick up your daughter and amuse her. However, don't feel that you have to be a one-woman entertainment centre all day long. The more you try to help your daughter now, and allow for her rather sensitive nature, the more enjoyment you will get from seeing her begin to relax and enjoy life knowing that the security of your arms is always near, should she need it.

The Fifth Month

YOUR BABY IS BEGINNING TO DISPLAY A VARIETY OF FACIAL EXPRESSIONS and sounds. You will find that you are recognising what he wants by means of a single look or glance.

Your baby will enjoy sitting up and observing everything that's going on around him, though he will still need to be supported as he can't yet balance himself. Trips out in the buggy to watch the world go by are an exciting adventure for him.

It is at this stage that many mothers will be thinking about returning to work. If this is the case for you, by now you will have researched which types of child-care provision suit you and your baby best. You can be sure that, provided you have done your homework and taken appropriate and thorough references, your baby will be well looked after. Make sure you allow enough time for your baby and carer to get to know each other and it is likely that you will need to establish a different approach to your work, whether it means altering your hours or simply leaving the office on time at the end of day.

Whatever your situation, you can be sure that your baby will benefit from having a happy and fulfilled mother – whether you have chosen to stay at home or return to the workplace.

Managing childcare

- A nanny will give you the most flexibility regarding working hours and will enable you to preserve your baby's home environment, which is the most familiar place for him. However, this is the most expensive option and not viable for many parents.

- Using a childminder can work out very well, as they are more than likely to be an experienced parent who is able to care for your baby in a warm family environment.

- Some parents are fortunate in that their child's grandparents are willing to help out and live close enough to take care of the baby on a regular basis.

- Whoever you decide to entrust your baby to, it is very important that you are meticulous about obtaining their professional and personal references.

- Your baby's carer will need management and support, no matter how good or experienced they are. These simple guidelines can contribute to the success of the arrangements.

Communicating with carers

- Draw up a contract detailing your carer's salary, as well as how and when it will be paid. You should also include the duration of paid holidays (and whether this includes bank holidays) and how much paid sick leave she is entitled to. It is also a good idea to outline notice periods for holidays so that you are able to arrange suitable cover in time, as well as a notice period should she decide to leave her job. Discuss every detail with your carer before drawing up the contract so that there is no confusion or misunderstanding.

- Make a list of what you expect your nanny to do – the routines, the outings, the household chores (washing the baby's clothes, but not the family laundry!) and the cooking arrangements. Discuss this in detail with your nanny, asking for their opinion and agreement. With a childminder, a list of your baby's routines, naps and feed times will be vital, and you must take time to sort out the practical issues, such as how his routines will fit in with the

In the evening, try to allow enough time to discuss your baby's day with his carer

other children they care for, who will provide nappies, food, etc.

- Always leave enough time at the beginning of the day for a calm and thoughtful hand over. It is distressing for your baby and unsettling for his carer if you are always late and rushing out of the door.

- Similarly, in the evening, try to allow enough time to discuss your child's day with his carer and for them to raise any issues or concerns. If this is not proving possible, particularly if you find yourself picking up a very tired child from a childminder at the end of the day, arranging a regular telephone call to discuss any concerns at an agreed time might be a more appropriate opportunity to talk.

- Give plenty of encouragement and be appreciative of her commitment and enthusiasm.

- If you have any concerns or reservations regarding the way your carer is looking after your baby, raise them immediately, but do so in a constructive and thoughtful manner. Criticism is de-motivating and unproductive. Provided you have given plenty of support, discussing your mutual concerns should strengthen your relationship rather than harm it.

TOP TIP
Do not be jealous of the affection between your baby and his carer. Your baby will not love you any less because he is learning to love someone else too. Your relationship with your baby, as his mother, is unassailable.

Nursery care

If you have chosen a nursery, you are sure to have done so having researched and personally visited all the day nurseries in your local area. Personal recommendations are worthwhile, but remember that what suits one baby may not suit the different personality of another.

- Look for a nursery with a friendly, caring environment and one that does not have a high turnover of staff – your baby should not have to keep getting to know new faces. Many nurseries have a 'key worker' scheme in which one or two selected carers will take special responsibility for your child. This makes it easier for him as he can begin to relate to the familiar faces he will see each day.

Leaving your baby for short trial sessions on a regular basis before you return to work will help him adjust to this situation

- Expect your baby to take a little longer to adapt to a nursery environment and, where possible, take steps to enable yourself to introduce him to his nursery gently. Leaving him for short trial sessions on a regular basis before you return to work will get him used to the new environment and will enable him to understand that you will always return to him at the end of the session. It will also help you to get used to leaving him.

- Don't be surprised if your baby finds the separation difficult at first. If you always use the same words when leaving him he will come to know the routine and realise that you will reappear again. In the beginning he may be a little tearful at being left each time. If you can build a friendly rapport with the staff, especially those directly involved with him, then he will learn to trust them as he sees you smiling and talking with them. Your body language and facial expressions will help him feel at ease. However you are feeling inside at the prospect of leaving him, by remaining cheerful,

TOP TIP
Try to make a point of keeping in touch with the mothers at your baby's nursery as this will help develop his social circle.

positive and smiling – particularly when saying goodbye – you will really help him get used to his new experience.

- As with any form of childcare, good communication and consideration are essential in forming a good relationship with the nursery staff.

Feeding

- Your baby should be established on five milk feeds a day, and the majority of babies will need the fifth late feed until solids are well established between six and seven months. However, there are some babies who may need to drop the late-night feed before solids are introduced if they begin to cut right back or refuse their first feed of the morning.

- If you find that your baby is losing interest in the first feed of the day, I would advise that you gradually reduce the amount he is having at the late-night feed. If he is breastfed, cut it back by a couple of minutes on each breast every couple of nights, until he is only taking two to three minutes on each side. Continue to give him this small feed for a few more nights. If he is still not very hungry, try cutting it out altogether. If he only manages to sleep through to 5am or 6am, it would be best to feed him straight away from one breast, and try to settle him back until 7am, rather than have him awake until then.

- If your baby is formula-fed, you can cut back the amount you give him by an ounce every couple of nights. If he continues to sleep through until 7am, and then takes a good feed, continue with a small feed at 10.30pm. However, if he is still fussy about the morning feed, then try cutting it out altogether. But, like the breastfed baby, he should be fed if he wakes early and then settled back to sleep.

- You may also find that you can cut out the late feed and he will sleep well for a couple of weeks until nearer 7am, and then start to wake earlier. If he is nearly six months old you should discuss with your health visitor whether you should re-introduce a fifth milk feed, or wean him slightly earlier.

- If your baby is totally breastfed and feeding five times a day, but still waking in the night and refusing to settle without a feed, it may be that the last feed of the day is not enough. You should try expressing some milk earlier in the day, so that you can offer it to him after the 10.30pm feed, to see if it will help him sleep later. If he is a very large baby, you should discuss with your health visitor whether you will need to introduce a small amount of solids.

Breastfeeding and returning to work

If you been expressing milk from early on, your baby will have become used to taking milk from an occasional bottle, so there should not be a problem once you return to work and he needs to take all his daily feeds from a bottle (see page 102 for guidelines on how to wean your baby on to a bottle).

Once at work, if you wish your baby to continue drinking breast milk during the day, you will need to express milk for him and store it for the following day's feeds. Hopefully, you will be able to breastfeed your baby as usual at the 7am and 6.15pm feeds, while expressing most of the milk he needs in your absence during the working day or in the late evening.

EXPRESSING EQUIPMENT
You will need to get used to using a hand-operated or battery-operated breast pump well before you go back to work, particularly if you are used to a larger electric expressing machine. You will also need to prepare a work bag that can take the required number of clean sterilised bottles, breast pump, breast pads and anything else you find useful. A spare shirt and bra could come in very handy!

Expressing at work

- Check with your employer well in advance of returning to work that there will be a quiet place available where you will be able to express. Also check that they are happy for you to store expressed milk in the refrigerator. It is worth knowing that employers are now required by law to provide suitable facilities, and the appropriate time, for breastfeeding mothers.

- Make sure that your child's carer is familiar with the storage and handling of breast milk.

- Once you return to work, it is essential that you pay particular attention to your diet and that you rest well in the evening. It would be advisable to continue expressing milk at 10pm to ensure that you maintain a good milk supply.

Sleeping

- Babies of five to six months of age need approximately three hours sleep between the hours of 7am and 7pm. This should be divided up into two to three naps a day.

- Babies who sleep well at lunchtime will probably manage to get through the afternoon without a nap, but if they sleep for a shorter time then they will need a short nap between 4pm and 5pm if overtiredness is to be avoided at bath and bedtime.

- If your baby has a short lunchtime nap, and refuses to sleep later on in the afternoon, then you would need to start the bath and bedtime routine slightly earlier to avoid him falling asleep on his feed after the bath.

- If you find that your baby is regularly cutting back on his lunchtime nap, then you should try reducing his morning nap to thirty minutes, to see if that helps him to sleep longer at lunchtime.

- If your baby is still feeding at 10.30pm or in the middle of the night or early morning, it is important to feed him and settle him quietly, without lots of talking and eye contact. This can be difficult if he wakes at 6am in the morning, as he may have had enough sleep and want to start the day. However, it is worth persevering and trying to get him back to sleep until 7/7.30am, if you do not want early morning waking to become a habit.

TOP TIP
Since you will be starting to go out to more play dates and activities during this stage, some of his morning naps can be taken in the car or in the buggy on the way to the event.

The bed and bathtime routine

Continue with the established bathtime routine and ensure your baby has his bath at 5.45pm each day and that he is massaged and dressed and ready for a feed at 6.15pm.

Development

Mental development

Your baby is becoming increasingly expressive and may demonstrate this with his physical movements. His pleasure at seeing you might be shown by a bout of vigorous bouncing. He is more likely to be shy with people he doesn't know, and more vocal in his attachment to his main carer. This can sometimes be difficult for the father, if he is seeing less of his baby. It is, however, a stage that passes quickly, and usually a baby of this age will adapt quickly to his father if his mother is away from him for any length of time.

- Your baby is becoming more self-aware, and will dislike being left out of conversations or general goings-on. He is learning to promote physical cuddles, and will lean in on you or try to embrace you.

- He will enjoy touching your face with his hand, and nuzzling you with his face. Hair pulling and patting is another favourite pastime.

Your baby is more likely to be shy with people he doesn't know, and more vocal in his attachment to his main carer

- His range of emotional responses is increasing with every day, and he is able to show love, humour, surprise, fear, suspicion, anger and a certain amount of determination.

- During this month, a baby will sometimes become attached to a particular comforter; this might be a muslin square or a toy.

- As long as you are close by or holding him he may still be happy to smile at strangers although separation anxiety can begin. He may hide his head into your shoulder or turn away when introduced to someone new. Although he likes new surroundings he will like to be close to you until he is used to them. He will smile and vocalise but normally to people he is familiar with.

Physical development

- Your baby might now be able to sit on his own unaided for a few minutes. Do be aware that he will fall backwards for quite a while before he has fully mastered his balance so be sure to keep him fully supported and supervised. The back of your baby's head is particularly vulnerable.

- Your baby will probably be able to roll on to his front, and then from his front on to his side.

Your baby might now be able to sit on his own unaided for a few minutes

Use cushions to help support your baby when she is sitting

Your baby may raise his arms to show you he wants to be picked up

- He might be able to wave, and some babies of this age will raise their arms to be picked up. Your baby might also be able to bring his feet to his mouth in an attempt to try to suck his toes.

- His control when reaching and picking things up is improving. He is far less likely to miss now when he reaches for something. His grasping has got better, but his ability to let go has not quite caught up.

- Your baby will have more head control and should now be able to hold his head steady. He may even begin leaning forward out of his bouncy chair, which can be quite alarming. A recent invention of a rounded seat that both supports and secures your baby may be worth investing in. Made from a soft lightweight material, the chair has no straps, as the sturdy design supports his back and holds him in a sitting position.

SAFETY

Your baby's fascination by all he sees around him means he will start to grab at things such as cloths and table covers, plants and anything else which is within his reach and looks interesting. Make sure there is nothing near by which he can grab and pull down on to himself. Be particularly aware of trailing leads from electrical items, such as kettles. Get down on to his level and see for yourself what he can reach or possibly put his fingers into. Never leave small items such as coins around on low tables, always use fireguards around heaters and working fireplaces and cover all accessible electrical sockets with plug-in covers.

Saying 'No'

You may find that your baby will begin to grab at hair, glasses and anything he can reach for but won't let go, despite you asking him to. Although the actual word 'No' won't mean anything to him, the tone of your voice certainly will. He will sense disapproval if you say it in a firm voice and, at the same time, gently prise his fingers from the offending place or object. Sometimes if 'No' is said just as he goes to grab at something, he will stop, as he prefers to hear approval in your voice. Likewise, a more positive way of preventing him from grabbing at an object is to distract him with another of his toys. Although you do not want to be saying 'No' constantly, there do need to be certain limits that he understands, particularly where safety is concerned. Provided you and other members of the family are consistent in the way you deal with these situations he will soon learn what is not acceptable.

Baby teeth and teething

On average a baby's teeth begin to appear at around five to seven months. However, occasionally a newborn is born with a tooth already showing, and at the opposite end of the scale, it is not a concern if your baby's teeth do not come through until he is a year old.

Teething symptoms

Contrary to common belief, teething should not cause feverishness nor tummy upsets (see page 131). But a tooth coming through may be temporarily painful for your child and his gums may appear slightly swollen. This can cause irritability and may be accompanied by a tendency to drool more than usual. If a rash develops around the mouth and chin, keep the area as dry as possible and use a very thin layer of barrier cream to prevent further inflammation.

Your child's teeth

- It is usual for the first tooth to come through at the bottom front of the mouth – a lower incisor, followed by a second lower incisor. Generally the next teeth to appear are the upper incisors, the top two middle teeth. The molars appear some time later along the sides and back of the mouth, followed by the canines. Finally the second molars in the upper and lower back of the mouth appear, usually by the second year. By the age of three your child should have a full set of 20 baby teeth.

FIRST TEETH The sensation of new teeth appearing can lead to a baby wanting to bite. Sometimes this can occur during feeding. To prevent this from happening, you should take the baby off the breast, saying firmly, 'No biting', as you do so. This should help him learn that biting you is wrong.

- It is really important to begin to clean your baby's teeth as soon as the first one appears. At this stage you will probably find it easiest to use a small piece of clean gauze wrapped round your finger, along with a small amount of special baby toothpaste which can be massaged all around the baby's gums and teeth. Later, when more teeth have appeared, you can move on to a soft baby toothbrush for cleaning.

- Clean your baby's tooth or teeth after breakfast and at bedtime, after he has had his milk. He will quickly get used to this and before long he will help you by trying to clean his teeth himself! There is a wide range of children's toothpastes on the market that have been specially formulated to protect your baby's teeth, while tasting nice.

Encouraging development through play

As your baby becomes more active, rolling and kicking, you may notice he goes through phases of getting frustrated. Because he still relies on you to provide for most of his needs he can become quite demanding of your attention. Knowing that this is a passing phase will help you to cope more effectively. Anticipate how long he will stay content for when on the floor kicking, and move him to somewhere different before frustration sets in.

- Make sure you have some suitable playthings in each room you use together. You can begin to make use of things you find around the house, provided that you check them carefully for sharp edges and remember that they will all probably end up in his mouth. Use everyday household items

Holding your baby's hands while she tries to push himself up on your legs will help her physical development but she will also enjoy the game

that are safe for him to explore, such as unbreakable egg cups, drinks mats or coasters, napkin rings, clean tea towels, spoons of plastic, wood or metal, a ring of measuring cups or spoons, cake and bun tins. Keep these things in a special basket and change them regularly to keep his interest.

- When on your knee your baby will probably love to push up to a standing position and begin to take all his weight on his legs while holding your

Continue to play and sing with your baby on a daily basis

hands, and this is a fun game for both of you to play. When he is kicking he will now have his legs fully up in the air and will play as much with his toes as he does with his hands.

- Before your baby becomes fully mobile you may want to start to use a playpen, if you have not done so already. Put him in it for short periods now, with a few toys to interest him. An activity centre should be secured safely on the side, plus an assortment of toys will keep him occupied. Getting him used to being in a playpen before he is able to really move around will help you in a few months' time when you can use it to keep him safe should you need to be out of his sight for a few minutes.

- Your baby is beginning to learn to look for something that has dropped from his sight, but he will also let go of one toy if another is given to him. He is able to concentrate for longer when something really interests him,

but still relies on you to provide him with new and exciting things to play with so boredom and frustration don't set in.

Toys, games and books

- Continue to play and sing with your baby on a daily basis introducing a few more action songs such as 'Tommy Thumb', 'Pat-a-cake' and 'Row, row, row the boat'. Continue to play games of 'Peekaboo', which can sometimes help a baby who is becoming slightly anxious about you leaving a room.

- As well as his board and soft books you may like to make him his own photo album. There are special baby albums that are made from fabric and which have clear pockets for photos to be inserted into. Find pictures of people he knows, such as grandparents or older cousins who he doesn't see so frequently, as well as you and your partner and, of course, himself.

- Find board books that have single photos of objects he knows such as a book, a ball, a bottle and a teddy. Look at them together and help him to realise that each object has a name by asking him, 'Where's the ball? Show me'. He may not yet physically show you by pointing but he will look at the right picture. Praise him for doing so.

- As well as all the toys he already has your baby will be ready for more complex activity centres, cubes and boards. If he has one of these already you may notice that he is able to work out the more complex actions now. Show him a new action once or twice, then leave him to discover how to work the buttons and dials by himself. It may take him a while but will be a valuable learning experience.

TOP TIP
At bathtime, provide your baby with toys that can pour or be filled as well as empty shampoo bottles and plastic soap dishes that he will find just as interesting.

Q&A

sitting and teething

Q

How can I get my baby to sit alone safely? Even with cushions on the floor, I am afraid she will topple over and hurt her head.

A

To help your daughter sit unaided, she needs plenty of practice and encouragement from you. Spending lots of time on her tummy from an early age will have helped her lift her neck and strengthen her back muscles. By four months, she should be able to do mini press-ups using her forearms to lift her head and shoulders off the ground.

Now your daughter is nearing six months, begin to place her within a circle of cushions, using a V-shaped cushion behind her, if you have one. Stay close by and make a game of catching her if she begins to topple. Her natural sitting position is on her bottom with her legs out at right angles, so much of her weight is on the backs of her thighs. The knees will be bent and often the soles of the feet touch. This is a good, balanced sitting posture, taking the strain off her lower back and allowing her to breathe well. To begin with, a baby will lean forward and use their hands and arms for support as they sit. By about

seven months, however, your daughter will be able to sit up and use her hands to hold toys and play. At this stage, her head control will allow her to look around without losing her balance.

Until you are sure she is well-balanced and able to twist and turn safely, keep her within her cushions and stay within reach. Any falls that do happen may surprise her but at least she will be falling into something soft. A gentle, 'All fall down, up we come' from you will take away any anxiety and she will probably be willing to try again. Do enjoy this stage, as encouraging your daughter to sit alone can be fun for both of you.

Q

My baby has recently cut his first tooth and he became very grizzly and upset when it was coming through. Is there anything I can do to prevent this happening when further teeth start arriving?

A

Some mothers do feel that their babies are much more irritable when a tooth is coming through. Although there are babies who never seem to suffer from teething, for those who do, it appears to be worse with the

first teeth. It is thought that babies adapt to the sensation of new teeth arriving and learn to live with it.

If your baby is really irritable when a tooth is coming through, you can try rubbing his gums with teething gel or giving him a sachet of homeopathic teething powder to ease the pain. Do not offer any other medication unless prescribed by your doctor. You could also get a plastic teething ring for him to bite down on. Try placing it in the refrigerator for a short while before giving it to him, to see if the cool sensation helps his sore gums.

If your baby develops a temperature, or goes off his food, or is sick, you should consult a doctor. All too often I hear of babies whose irritable symptoms have been put down to teething, when in fact it turns out to be an ear or throat infection.

The Sixth Month

THE SIXTH MONTH CAN OFTEN BE ONE OF THE MOST HECTIC FOR MANY mothers as it is a phase that sees the introduction of solids. Don't be daunted by the weaning stage. By being organised and carefully planning ahead, you can ensure your baby gets lots of healthy, home-cooked fresh foods and you will save yourself hours of extra time in the kitchen. Feeding times will initially take longer as your baby needs to learn how to eat solids from a spoon, so it is important that when planning your day during the next few weeks you allow enough time for the new feeding routines to become established.

Mealtimes should be enjoyable for both you and your baby, and they play a very important part in your baby's development. Try always to take the time to eat breakfast with your baby and, as his lunch moves to the later time of 12 noon, try to eat with him whenever possible. Once your baby is established on three meals a day, preparing lunches that are suitable for both you and your baby will, in the long run, save you time. When I worked with families I used to encourage both parents to have a 'big cook-up' every couple of weeks. Do not feel guilty about enlisting the help of your husband, family members or a close friend to get involved with this. It is amazing how many meals can be prepared in an evening, and how much less of a chore it becomes when you are working in a team.

Once your baby is sitting up well, you can begin to use a high chair at mealtimes

Feeding

By the time your baby reaches six months he will probably be having between four and five milk feeds a day, although some larger babies who are exclusively breastfed may still need a middle-of-the-night feed, especially if the 10pm feed is a smaller one. It is important that solids are introduced no later than six months, as by this time the iron store that your baby was born with will be getting very low.

Introducing solids

Government guidelines have changed in recent years, encouraging mothers to wait until their baby is six months before introducing solids. Previously, when solids were regularly introduced at four months, the advice was that a new food should be introduced every three to four days, and only after the baby had taken most of his milk feed. Because solids are now being introduced later this is no longer the case. You will need to work through the first-stage foods much more quickly and increase the amounts you give fairly rapidly so that your baby is well established on iron-rich foods, such as protein and pulses, by the time he is seven months. Choosing breakfast cereals and baby rice that are fortified with iron will also ensure that your baby receives adequate amounts of iron in his diet at this stage.

By seven months you should aim to have reduced your baby's milk intake to three milk feeds a day, and to have established him on a proper lunch and tea with a small breakfast.

Signs of being ready for weaning

If your baby is under six months of age and is showing all the signs below, it is vital you discuss things with your health visitor or GP and decide with them whether to wean early or not. The weaning guidelines I outline in this chapter are all aimed at babies who are being weaned at six months in accordance with the Department of Health (DoH) recommendations. If, however, you have been advised to wean early, you can find in-depth advice on how to do so in *The Contented Little Baby Book of Weaning*.

* He has been taking a full feed four or five times a day from both breasts or a 240ml (8oz) bottle of formula and has been happily going for four hours between feeds, but now gets irritable and chews his hands long before his next feed is due.

* He has been taking a full feed from both breasts or a 240ml (8oz) formula feed and screams for more the minute the feed finishes.

* He usually sleeps well at night and nap times but is starting to wake up earlier and earlier or in the middle of the night looking for a feed.

* He is chewing his hands excessively, displaying eye-to-hand coordination and trying to put things into his mouth.

* If your baby is showing all the above signs but your health visitor or GP

has advised you not to wean him early, it is important to remember that your baby may need an extra feed in the middle of the night until solids are introduced.

How to prepare your baby's first foods

- Ensure all kitchen surfaces and equipment are scrupulously clean. Surfaces can be wiped with anti-bacterial cleaner and kitchen towel, which is more hygienic than cloths.

- All feeding equipment should be sterilised for the first six months. Sterilise ice cube trays or freezer containers by boiling them in a large saucepan of water for five minutes. Smaller items such as spoons and serving bowls can be put in the steam steriliser, if you have one. Wash cooking utensils in a dishwasher or rinse handwashed items with boiling water from the kettle.

- Fruit and vegetables should be peeled and any cores, pips or blemishes removed. They should be rinsed thoroughly with filtered water.

- Steam or cook the fruit or vegetables in filtered water until soft, then purée. If using a food processor, check the mixture carefully for lumps. Mix to a soft smooth consistency (like yoghurt) with some of the cooking water. Do not add salt, sugar or honey.

- Freshly prepared food should be cooled and stored in the fridge or freezer in ice cube trays (see page 139) as soon as possible.

- Food should always be heated thoroughly to ensure that any bacteria are killed. Any leftover food should be discarded, never reheated and used again.

- When batch cooking, take out a portion of food for your baby to eat now and freeze the rest.

 **FIRST FOODS**
The following foods are all excellent first tastes of solids:

organic baby rice	potato
pear	green beans
apple	courgettes
carrot	swede
sweet potato	

Once your baby is happily taking these foods, you can introduce the following:

oats	avocado
parsnips	barley
mango	peas
peaches	cauliflower
broccoli	

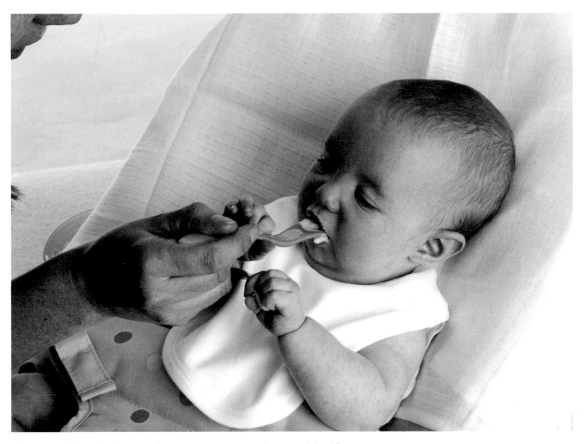

Baby rice is the best food to start the weaning process as it has a very bland flavour

- If using prepared baby food, transfer food to a dish, never feed straight from the jar. As with fresh food, never reheat leftovers.

- Be sure to test the temperature of your baby's food before feeding him as it will need time to cool down. Using a separate spoon, touch a tiny amount to your lips to check it is not too hot. Stir the food well to ensure that it is the same temperature all the way through and that there are no 'hot spots'.

The first 'meal'

- Introduce solids at the 11am feed. Offer your baby only half his milk feed first so that he is hungry enough to accept the solids, then offer him a tea-spoonful of pure organic baby rice mixed to a smooth consistency using expressed milk, formula milk or cooled freshly boiled water.

- If your baby is on five or six milk feeds a day but is not showing any interest in the solids at 11am despite only taking half his milk feed first, it would be advisable to try offering the solids before the milk.

- Place a rounded plastic feeding spoon just far enough into his mouth and gently bring the spoon up and out against the roof of his mouth, his upper gums will take the food off, which will encourage him to feed. He will very soon learn to take the food from the spoon.

- When finished, offer him the second half of his milk feed.

- Aim to gradually decrease the amount of milk that you offer before his solids. If breastfeeding, continue to reduce the time he is on the breast by 2–3 minutes each day. If your baby is formula-fed, then reduce his feed by 30ml (1oz) every couple of days. This will encourage him to take more solid food, and will also gradually decrease the amount of milk he is taking after the solids.

- Continue to decrease the milk he is taking at 11am until he is happy to start with his solids at lunchtime. Once he is taking 4–6 cubes (one cube is approximately equal to one tablespoon), he should have cut the amount of milk he is taking after the solids until he is taking a few minutes on the breast or a couple of ounces of formula.

- Once he is takingsix cubes you should then start to introduce small amounts of protein at lunchtime. Begin by replacing two of the vegetable cubes with a cube of a protein recipe that is easy to digest, such as chicken or lentil casserole.

- Continue to replace a cube of vegetables each day with a cube of a protein, until his lunch consists of a balanced meal (protein, vegetable and a carbohydrate, such as potato or sweet potato).

Introducing different tastes

After a couple of days, once your baby is established on baby rice, introduce a small amount of pear purée, mixing it with the baby rice.

If he tolerates the pear, small amounts of organic fruits and vegetables (see

First Foods list, page 136) can now be introduced. To prevent your baby developing a sweet tooth, try to give more vegetables than fruit. Increase the servings by one cube every couple of days. Once he is taking 4 to 6 cubes he should have cut the amount of milk he is taking after the solids until he is only taking a few minutes on the breast or a couple of ounces of formula.

Teatime

Within a couple of days of introducing baby rice at lunchtime, you should progress to introducing solids in the evening as well. Move the baby rice and fruit to teatime and introduce a variety of different vegetables at lunchtime. Try to increase the baby rice at teatime by one teaspoonful every couple of days.

Breakfast

> ### FREEZING BABY FOOD
> • Cooked puréed food should be covered as quickly as possible and transferred to the freezer as soon as it is cool. Never put warm food in the refrigerator or freezer.
> • Ice cube trays are very useful as they enable you to freeze small portions of food. Wash and sterilise, fill with purée and open-freeze till solid. Pop the ice cubes out of the tray and into a sterilised plastic box. Seal well, label and freeze. Use foods within six months and never refreeze cooked food.
> • Defrost frozen (covered) food in the refrigerator overnight, or leave at room temperature if you forget, transferring it to the fridge as soon as it has defrosted. Heat as usual.
> • Always use defrosted foods within 24 hours.

A baby is ready to start having breakfast once he shows signs of hunger long before his 11am feed. This usually happens between the ages of six and seven months (and when the late feed is dropped). Organic oatmeal cereal with a small amount of puréed fruit is a favourite with many babies. You should still give your baby most of his milk feed first; after a couple of weeks give about two-thirds of his milk feed first, then the cereal, finishing with the remainder of the milk.

By the age of seven months you should aim to have reduced your baby's milk feeds to three a day – this will help increase his appetite and establish three solids meals a day. As you increase his solids, you should find that he automatically cuts down and eventually refuses his late feed, should he still be having it. Between six and seven months your baby should have tasted most of the foods on the first stage list on page 136.

For in-depth advice on weaning and easy-to-follow feeding plans, please refer to *The Contented Little Baby Book of Weaning*.

Carrot and sweet potato are good first foods to offer as they are sweet in flavour but do not have the sugar content of fruit

WEANING TIPS
• **Prepare everything you will need in advance:** a baby chair if you are using one, bib, spoon, bowl and a clean, damp cloth.
• **Keep a food diary** to help you remember how your baby reacts to each new food. If your baby spits a food out or refuses it, it may not mean he dislikes it so try again in a week's time.
• **Once your baby is sitting up well,** begin to use a high chair at meal times. Having a tray or table in front of him will give him plenty of opportunity to feed himself. Always remember to strap him in and never leave him unsupervised. His hands should also be washed before and after the meal.

Avoid introducing dairy products, wheat, eggs, nuts and citrus fruit, as they are the foods most likely to trigger allergies. Honey should not be introduced before one year because of the risk of bee allergy.

Second-stage foods

When beginning weaning at the age of six months you will need to progress quickly though the first-stage foods so that iron-rich meat and vegetarian products can be introduced regularly.

The first sources of iron are found in lentils, broccoli and iron-rich breakfast cereals. Protein should be introduced by the seventh month in the form of lentils, poultry, fish and meat. However, your baby should be capable of digesting reasonable amounts of other solids before taking protein.

Check that all the bones are removed and trim off any fat or skin. Try cooking small amounts of chicken, meat or fish in a casserole with familiar root vegetables at first so that your baby does not find the taste too strong. Pulse the casserole in a food processor. Always introduce protein at lunchtime as it is harder to digest than carbohydrate.

Provided you do not have a history of allergies in the family, wheat-based cereals, pasta and bread can also be introduced.

Between the age of six and seven months your baby should become established on two to three servings of carbohydrates daily, in the form of cereal, wholemeal bread, pasta or potatoes. He should also have three servings of vegetables or fruit each day and one serving of animal or vegetable protein. A very hungry baby could have milk pudding or yoghurt after his tea.

> ### LEARNING TO DRINK FROM A BEAKER
> It can take time for a baby to learn how to drink from a beaker. Offer a drink from a beaker every day, to encourage your baby. You may need to try with several different types before finding one that suits him. The best are either ones with no handles at all, which are small enough for your baby to hold, or a double-handled type for two hands. The spout should be of the simple types with one or several holes, but no 'anti-drip' valve. This will mean that, if upturned, the beaker will leak but your baby will find it easier to drink. He may also find it easier to sip from a cup with no lid or spout.

Drinks

Your baby still needs a minimum of 600ml (20oz) of milk a day in his milk feeds. Once protein is introduced at lunchtime, the drink of milk should be replaced with a small drink of well-diluted juice or cooled boiled water from a baby beaker. Most babies of six months are capable of sipping and swallowing and this should be encouraged. By the age of one he should be taking all his milk and other drinks from a beaker.

Messy feeding

Introducing solids is another step towards helping your baby become more independent. It is important that you do not try to restrict his interest in solids by trying to keep him clean throughout the meal. Dressing your baby in clothes that are easy to wash and dry is very important at this stage, as is wearing the right bibs. I always advise using cloth bibs for this reason – they are easy to clean as you just put them straight into the wash. Mealtimes should be a pleasure for your baby and something he looks forward to. If he is to learn eventually to feed himself, getting in a mess is all part of the learning process.

Sleeping

- Babies of six to seven months of age need approximately two and a half to three hours sleep between the hours of 7am and 7pm.

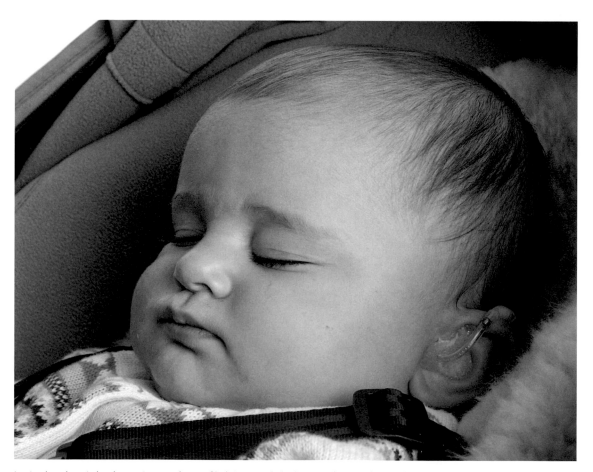

Letting her sleep in her buggy is a good way of helping your baby learn to sleep in places other than her own cot

- This should ideally be divided into two separate naps, a short nap in the morning and a longer one after lunch.

- By this age your baby will manage to stay awake longer than two hours at a time and will probably go down for his morning nap around 9.30am. This means that you should push the lunchtime nap nearer to 12.30/12.45pm, which will allow you to establish lunch at around 12 noon. He should then manage to get through the rest of the day without any more sleep.

- If you find that your baby is sleeping less than two hours at lunchtime he will probably need to have a short nap in the late afternoon, so that he is not overtired for bathtime and his last feed.

- If he is to sleep through from 7pm to 6/7am without a late feed, the last feed of the day becomes the 6.15pm feed, so it is important that he is not too tired to take a really good feed at this time.

> **TOP TIP**
> If you find your baby is getting very overtired before his bedtime you may need to bring his routine forward by 10–15 minutes for a short time.

Going out

If you have not already done so I would advise that you do arrange for your baby to have occasional lunchtime naps away from his own cot. It is important that he learns to sleep in other places, otherwise holidays and visits can become difficult if you have a baby who will only sleep in his own cot. Having lunch at a friend's house, and settling him in a travel cot there, or going out for occasional lunches and allowing him to sleep in his buggy is a good way of teaching him to adapt to sleeping elsewhere. If he does not sleep so long, just accept that he will need a short nap later on in the afternoon, so that he does not become overtired.

It is important that your baby learns to sleep in other places, otherwise holidays and visits can become difficult if you have a baby who will only sleep in his own cot

The bed and bathtime routine

Your baby will really love his bath at this age, and bathtime should become one of the most fun times of the day. He will enjoy a variety of different bath toys and will be able to sit up in one of the specially designed plastic bath seats that will allow him to play with his toys much more. Never leave your baby unattended in one of these bath seats – not even for a matter of seconds.

Hair washing

Washing your baby's hair becomes more of an issue at this age, particularly as he will have much more of it. He will also be enjoying more messy play and may be trying to feed himself. Some babies need their hair washed every night, and can get quite cross about it. I would advise you to get the hair washing over with as quickly as possible, so that the rest of the bath can be enjoyed. If you leave hair washing until the end, you risk lifting a screaming baby out of the bath, who then has to be dried, massaged and dressed.

SEPARATION ANXIETY

By this age you may begin to notice the signs of separation anxiety. Your baby may not be so willing to go to people he is unfamiliar with. He may turn away and bury his face when people come too close to him, although a smiling and friendly voice will bring him around to look at them, provided you stay close. He may begin to object when you leave the room or are out of sight. Once a baby realises that you can disappear from sight and he is not able to follow you he may become rather clingy and demanding. Playing lots of games of 'Peekaboo' and gradually moving further from him, hiding behind chairs and then the door of the room may help him feel more reassured. This phase can take a while to pass and is best dealt with sympathetically, scooping him up to take him with you if he does become distressed when he is unable to see you.

Development

Mental development

Your baby is now able to concentrate for longer periods of time. He is developing his ability to watch and imitate. He will follow you with his eyes, and endeavour to involve himself in your activities.

- Your baby will be babbling constantly now. You will find that he is beginning

Your baby may get nervous around people she is not familiar with and bury her face to hide away from them

Her increasing control will enable her to hold a toy with both hands

to respond to his name, and also can associate the words 'Mummy' and 'Daddy' to his parents. He will like to repeat sounds over and over again. There will be certain noises that he can associate with certain actions. He will be mouthing 'Ga, ga, ga', 'Ma, ma, ma', 'Da, da, da', 'Ba,ba,ba' .

• His developing cries have more pitch to them, and his language includes a more nasal sound. He will try to mimic inflections of tone and might begin to demonstrate a musical ability by humming or seeming to sing.

• The urge to explore 'cause and effect' is increasing. If your baby is aware that he can make a certain noise, he will enjoy repeating it again and again. His mental development is encouraging his physical independence. He might want to feed himself or hold his own bottle.

Physical development

By six months your baby is gaining a great deal of control over his hands. He now can reach out and grasp toys and objects, pulling them towards himself.

• He will also use both hands when holding a toy, and move it from one hand to the other. He will begin to develop a pincer grip, using finger and thumb to pick up small objects. Rather than just holding and mouthing toys he actually plays with them, exploring all the possibilities they offer.

• He will enjoy his first attempts to feed himself.

• His increasing strength in his arms and upper body enables him to take more of his weight and some babies will attempt to crawl at this stage. Your baby may begin to sit for short spells at this stage unaided, although it will be quite a while before he is safe to sit without cushions behind him.

- You may notice your baby making attempts to crawl by the end of this month. He may begin to draw one knee up to his tummy. Encourage him when he shows signs of crawling by placing toys just out of his reach, or by rolling balls or toy cars near to him. Some babies manage to move quite well by pushing round on their tummies to get where they want. He may also roll to places he wishes to explore. Once you realise he is able to move a little, be prepared to use a playpen when having to leave the room for a short while, such as when answering the door. Once your baby has worked out that he can reach places, he will begin to move at quite a speed and may get into trouble within a short space of time. Provided he has been used to being in the playpen before he was mobile, he should not object to short periods of time spent there.

Encouraging development through play

During this month your baby may learn to let go of a toy and follow with his eyes the path to where it has fallen. Dropping toys for you to retrieve is a game which most babies love. If this game becomes too much and you feel that you spend all your time retrieving toys for your baby, you may want to buy one of the specially designed toys that can be attached to his chair or buggy. Show him how to retrieve them by himself. You may need to show

Placing toys out of her reach will encourage her to crawl

She may choose to roll to move around and reach for objects

him several times before he is able to do this for himself. Stay close by if you decide to use these toys to make sure he doesn't have an accident. Remember to remove any of the toys before leaving him to sleep if they are in his buggy or cot.

- Use your baby's name regularly. Lift him to see himself in the mirror and then say his name – 'Who's that? That's Harry'. Repeat his name in relation to objects. 'Where's Harry's truck?' 'This is Harry's cup'.

- If your baby is able to sit alone for short periods, provide plenty of cushions around him as he is still likely to topple both forwards and backwards. Place one or two toys to each side of him as he becomes more proficient at sitting. This will encourage him to turn his body and reach out to get the toy. Once he is sitting well, a whole new world opens up for your baby. He will be able to use both hands to manipulate his toys, allowing him to discover more about how they work.

- Once your baby is able to take the weight of his body fully on his legs he will enjoy bouncing up and down on your knee, being held in the standing position. If he enjoys doing this you can begin to use a baby bouncer that is suspended from a doorframe. Limit his time to around 20 minutes for each session and always remain close by.

Toys, games and books

Now is the time to introduce wooden building blocks. Choose sets that have small wooden cubes as well as other shapes. These will be used for many months and years to come. Once he is able to hold a toy in each hand, encourage your baby to have a small cube in each hand and bang them together. Show him how to build towers, placing one brick on top of each other. It will take time for him to learn this skill but he will delight in knocking down the towers you build for him.

- Encourage his hand coordination with clapping games such as 'Pat-a-cake'.

- Use his love of sounds to introduce animal noises when looking at books together. He may try to copy you and will love to be encouraged in his attempts. Blowing bubbles or raspberries will amuse him and, although it can be messy during mealtimes, this is all part of the development of his mouth and jaw to prepare him for talking.

- There are many books suitable for this age: simple board books, 'feely' books, simple stories and books of objects, both in photographs and drawings. Around this age you may like to start looking at one or two books together before he settles to sleep at night as part of his bedtime routine.

- One way to widen the selection of books you show him is to use your local library. Most will issue tickets for a baby of six months and above, some may even allow him to have a ticket before this. A weekly trip to the library to change the books is a good way to spend an afternoon. Many libraries hold 'Story and Rhyme' sessions that you may like to attend. Libraries are increasingly aware of how important it is to develop a love of books in the very young. For this reason, most libraries encourage children's events. Children's noise is acceptable, so you need not worry if your baby is making a lot of noise.

Your baby will love to copy your actions: encourage this with lots of games

Board books with simple stories are suitable at this age

Classes and activities

Your library is also a good place to find out about local activities which may be on offer once your baby is six months old. There are many types of music groups that offer classes for this age. Most of these will offer a free introductory session. This will enable you to try out several before deciding which is best suited to you and to your baby's needs. Small classes are usually best for this age, lasting no longer than 30–45 minutes.

Gymnastic type classes are also popular once your baby is showing signs of beginning to move. These usually incorporate some kind of singing, which your baby will enjoy, even if he is not quite ready to join in all the physical activities.

Q&A

starting nursery

Q

My six-month-old son is starting nursery in a fortnight's time and I am worried about how he will adapt to eating and sleeping there. I also want to make sure that he stays in his current routine for the four days he is at home.

He is in a contented little baby routine and has been a very easy child. He is used to having his lunch at 12.15pm, however at nursery this will be earlier, at 11.45am. Tea is at 3.45pm (usually 5.30pm at home). He currently has his afternoon milk at about 3pm so I am sure he will not be hungry for his tea at nursery.

At nursery, they have a separate cot area for sleeping, which he will share with six other babies, but it will be noisier and lighter than home. I am sure he will not sleep as well as he does normally.

Can you please suggest how I change his routine to ensure he keeps to a 7.30pm bedtime? I will be able to pick him up around 5pm initially so he will be able to have a short nap in the car.

Any ideas or tips you can give me on how to help adjust his routine for nursery would be much appreciated.

A

Many mothers are initially concerned about how their baby will cope with eating and sleeping alongside other babies when they have been used to the quiet of home. Most babies adapt amazingly well. Initially, you may find he does not sleep at nursery quite as long at lunchtime as he does at home, but this may lengthen once he grows used to the different noises and sights of nursery. Be aware that during the first few weeks, however well he sleeps at nursery, he may well be tired when he returns. The adjustments he needs to make, the new surroundings and people are a lot for him to take in. Although you are eager for him to remain with his 7.30pm bedtime, in the first weeks after starting nursery you may need to make this earlier until he is more settled. As he will not be at nursery every day you can adjust bedtime depending on what has happened earlier in the day. On the days he is at home you can remain on your present routine if it suits you. Once he has got used to being at nursery he will probably manage to have a 7.30pm bedtime every night.

With regard to his feeding, the milk he has at 3pm could become part of his nursery tea at the slightly later time of 3.45pm. Once home, offer him a healthy snack. such as mini-sandwiches, thick soups, simple pasta dishes etc. How much of this he will eat is an unknown. It is something you will only be able to gauge as you get into the nursery routines. If he is tired and picky, try not to push him too hard even if you feel he has not eaten well at nursery. Sometimes babies of this age refuse all food but will happily take a bowl of cereal in the evening.

Remember, that if he has had a good lunch and early tea at nursery, he cannot be expected to eat another full meal when he gets home. All that is needed is a small snack to get him through to bedtime happily. Be careful of offering him so much food that he reduces his bedtime milk feed. A full milk feed at bedtime is still important at this age to help him sleep through the night. As long as he continues to sleep well at night, you should find that he will adapt to the various changes of his daytime routine.

The Seventh Month

THIS MONTH CAN OFTEN BE ONE OF THE BUSIEST MONTHS OF YOUR baby's first year. Babies of this age tend to get bored very quickly and crave lots of attention and company. Remember, outings do not always have to be baby-orientated.

Your baby will now be established on three meals a day, but it will still be a little time before he can properly join in with the family meals. As with a six-month-old, try to plan most of your baby's meals in advance so that it leaves you plenty of time to get out and about during the day.

Although it will be difficult, try to fit in a little 'me time' every day as it is important to look after yourself, both physically and mentally. The majority of gyms now have a baby crèche, so do not feel guilty about leaving him there twice or three times a week to enable you to join an exercise class or have a swim. If you do not have family close at hand who can take the baby off your hands for a morning or afternoon every now and again, try to set up a babysitting circle with other mothers, so that you can all take turns in having a morning or afternoon to yourselves occasionally. You will feel better for it and will have more energy for the rest of the day's activities with your baby.

Feeding

- Your baby should now be established on three solid meals and three milk feeds a day.

- He should not need feeding at 10.30pm or in the middle of the night. However, if you are exclusively breastfeeding and your milk supply is low later in the day, it is possible that he may wake up in the night because he is not getting enough milk to drink at his 6.15pm feed.

- If your baby is still waking in the night or very early in the morning, it is most certainly worth trying a top-up feed after the 6.15pm feed, with some milk that you have expressed earlier in the day.

- Formula-fed babies still need 530–600ml (18–20oz) of milk per day, inclusive of milk used in cooking. Milk feeds should be before breakfast, in the afternoon and at bedtime.

Replace his lunchtime milk with a beaker of cool boiled water or well-diluted juice

Drinks

By the end of seven months your baby's milk at lunchtime should be replaced with a drink of cooled boiled water or well-diluted juice from a beaker. At mealtimes it is best to offer your baby water or juice after he has eaten most of his solids; that way the edge will not be taken off his appetite.

Progressing with solids

- During the seventh month foods need not be so puréed and, apart from chicken and meat, you should start to get your baby used to taking some of his food mashed or pulsed. Fruit can be served raw but grated or mashed.

- Many babies are ready to accept stronger-tasting foods and they will take pleasure from different textures, colours and presentation.

- Breakfast should now be established. A cereal that is rich in iron and vitamins, plus mashed fruit, is ideal. Offer two-thirds of his milk feed first.

- At seven months your baby should be eating two to three servings of carbohydrates, three servings of fruit and vegetables, one serving of animal protein, or two of vegetable protein, every day.

First finger foods

- You should start to introduce small amounts of finger foods at this age. Raw soft pieces of fruit or lightly cooked vegetable batons, low-sugar rusks and fingers of lightly buttered toast are ideal.

- At this age the finger foods are likely to be sucked and squeezed rather than eaten, but this is all good training for later.

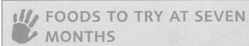 **FOODS TO TRY AT SEVEN MONTHS**

Fruit and vegetables

Apricots, melons, plums, peppers, pumpkin, cabbage, spinach, celery and tomatoes.

Protein sources

Red lentils, butter beans and other pulses. Chicken, cod, haddock (unsmoked) and lamb.

Dairy products

Yoghurt, milk puddings and mild full-fat cheese in cooking.

Olive oil can now be used in cooking and, by the eighth month, a small amount of herbs can be added.

- Your baby will be becoming more adept at picking up smaller pieces of food. Offer him a selection of steamed vegetables cut into dice or batons, small pieces of cheese, baby rice cakes, fingers of toast and pieces of suitable fruit.

Low-sugar rusks are a good first finger food

- As well as offering finger foods, encourage your baby to hold his own spoon and try to feed himself. This stage of self-feeding can be messy but it is a crucial part of his development and should be encouraged. He may need help to get his spoon into his mouth without turning it over, but the more he is allowed to try, the quicker he will learn.

- Never leave your baby alone while eating and always supervise him carefully.

Sleeping

- Babies of seven to eight months of age need approximately two and a half to three hours sleep between the hours of 7am and 7pm. This should be divided up into two separate naps, ideally with the longer one after lunch.

- You may find that your baby is starting to sleep a little later in the morning. If this is the case, and he is perhaps sleeping through to around 8am, he may no longer need a morning nap. However, you may have to bring his lunch forward slightly and allow him to sleep a little longer after lunch.

- At this age he may start to roll over and prefer to sleep on his tummy. When this happens, it would be a good idea to remove his sheet and blankets to prevent him from becoming tangled up in them. However, in the winter months this would mean replacing his lightweight sleeping bag with a warmer one to compensate for the lack of blankets.

Work and adjusting baby's bedtime

If you have returned to work you may want to try putting your baby to bed a little later, as you may not be getting home until the early evening. Although he will probably have dropped his late-afternoon nap by now, you could ask his carer to try leaving him to sleep slightly longer at lunchtime, or encouraging him to have a short nap again in the late afternoon. This should allow you to push his bedtime on until 7.30/8pm. I would be very careful about allowing him to stay up any later, as babies of this age can suddenly start to wake up in the night again if they go to sleep in an overtired state.

> **DIFFERENT BEDTIMES**
> You may find that you have to have different routines on the days you work to the ones you have when you are at home. As long as the bed and bathtime routine remains the same, he should manage to cope with going to bed slightly later on the days that you are working, while going to bed at the usual time on the days that you are at home - as long as you remember to adjust his daytime sleep accordingly.

Teething

If your baby's teeth have started to appear, he will constantly want to be chewing on something. Offering him finger foods at every meal will help and he may also prefer to have some of his solids served cold or cool while he is cutting a tooth. You can also try offering him one of the specially designed teething rings to chew on. Remember that teeth cleaning, every morning and every evening, should be introduced as part of his daily routine.

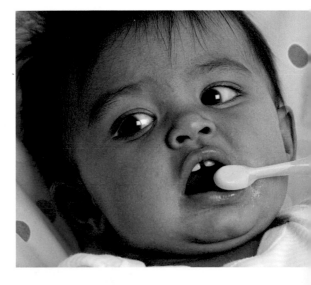

When teething, some babies tend to drool much more than normal and develop a rash around their mouth and chin, which can become inflamed and painful. It is important to keep the area as dry as possible If necessary, use a barrier cream to stop the skin becoming broken and inflamed.

> **EASING TEETHING PAIN**
> If your baby becomes grizzly or appears to be really irritable when a tooth is coming through you can try rubbing his gums with teething gel or giving him a sachet of homeopathic teething powder to ease the pain. Do not offer any other medication unless prescribed by your doctor. If he develops a temperature, or goes off his food, or is sick, you should consult a doctor. All too often I hear of babies whose irritable symptoms have been put down to teething, when in fact it turns out to be an ear or throat infection.

Development

Mental development

Your baby's coordination is improving and he continues to be more expressive. He will start to show to show his displeasure or frustration. He is more determined to reach objects out of range, and may shout with anger if things are removed from him.

- He will demonstrate his ability to concentrate by playing for longer with one specific toy. His manual dexterity will be improving and he will be starting to work out how simple toys operate.

- You may notice that he begins to pat at his own face and yours. He may also pat at faces in a book or his own reflection in a mirror. When patting your face it seems as if your baby is beginning physically to express his affection for you – although you may have to show him how to do it gently. Even at this young age, it is possible to direct his physical behaviour and you can teach him that he must be gentle with other people and pets. Repeatedly take his hand and stroke it against your face or his own.

- He is learning to differentiate between tones of voice much more now. He is probably already aware of the tone of your voice when you want him to stop doing something and say 'No' firmly, but increasingly he will understand a happy or sad voice. He will be aware of both praise and enthusiasm so try to use both as much as you can when talking to him.

- Your baby should be able to amuse himself for short periods throughout the day as well as enjoying playing with you. He will be more interested in other babies now and, if sitting near by, will reach towards them. He may both grab and coo at them but there will be little other interaction, apart from watching what they are doing.

Physical development

When on his tummy your baby will be able to balance on one arm and play with a toy in the other. He may be able to get up on his knees and hands and rock backwards and forwards, or he may start pulling his knees up towards his tummy. If so, he is showing signs of developing crawling skills, and safety around the home will become more of an issue (see page 163).

If your baby pulls his knees up to his tummy he may be showing early signs of wanting to crawl

At seven months your baby will be stronger and will be more capable of taking his own weight

- When held to standing he will be more capable of taking all his weight when held under the arms.

- He is using his hands now to investigate every possibility his toys can offer, pulling and tugging at them. He will shake, bang and rattle them constantly to see what they do. You may notice he uses his fingers now to grasp at toys, rather than using his whole palm. This 'pincer' movement may be further refined by the end of the month as he practises picking up smaller items.

- As your baby develops his handling skills he is far less likely to drop his toys accidentally, but may still enjoy letting them go and then getting you to retrieve them. He will now be able to hold on to one toy with one hand when handed another, rather than dropping the first.

- Your baby should be able to focus on small objects, and judge the distance to be able to reach to pick them up.

Encouraging development through play

- As well as constantly babbling to himself your baby may begin to initiate 'conversations' with you by making sounds. He may start to respond to you when you say, 'Look at that!' When singing familiar songs your baby may try to join in with you. Your baby will love games that involve blowing raspberries and tickling. He may try blowing raspberries himself, especially while eating.

- During this month separation anxiety can become more marked. Continue to play games of 'Peekaboo' especially where you can involve him. If you hide a favourite toy beneath a cloth and then ask him where it is, he may try to uncover the toy, especially if you leave a small part of the toy visible. Hide yourself behind a newspaper or muslin and encourage him to find you by pulling the paper or cloth away. He

You may notice he now uses his fingers to grasp at toys, rather than using his whole palm

understands that, despite not being able to see you or his toy, things don't disappear completely and will return once uncovered.

Toys, games and books

- With his increasing dexterity your baby will start to enjoy toys such as nesting cups and simple stacking cones. Although not yet able to stack the cups or arrange the cones in the right order, he will spend a great deal of time trying. Try not to always show him what to do, or rearrange his toys into the 'correct' order. Part of his learning will come from exploring all the possibilities for himself.

- Balls of all kinds will now be enjoyed. Use soft fabric ones inside the house and show your baby how to roll these. Once he can sit alone, sit in front of him and roll a ball to him. Encourage him to roll it back to you. Once he is up on his knees and attempting to crawl, a rolling ball will give him something to move towards.

- Moving toys such as simple cars, trucks and trains will begin to be of interest to your baby. By now he may have a favourite toy or comforter that he takes to bed with him, but also encourage him to play with teddies and soft toys. As his feelings of sadness, happiness and attachment begin to grow, he will use his soft toys in many ways. Choose ones with friendly faces, securely attached features and made from fabrics you will be able to wash or wipe.

- Continue to look at books at different times throughout the day. Make the connections with the pictures on the page and your baby. Show him a picture such as a cup, say the word, then ask 'Where's your cup?' and see if he looks to where it is. Begin to run your finger under any text and show him how to turn the pages. This shows him how books work.

As his feelings of sadness, happiness and attachment begin to grow, he will use his soft toys in many ways

Safety in the home

The most important time to child-proof your home is before your baby begins to crawl. Your home environment offers more hazards to your baby than the garden or a park. The familiarity of your surroundings contributes to the risks since we are most relaxed and off-guard in our home environments and can be distracted by the telephone or the doorbell ringing.

Taking a few hours to child-proof your home at this stage can eliminate many of the dangers for your crawling baby.

Your doctor's surgery will have information giving you further safety advice, however, here are a few tips:

- Be prepared to invest in some sensible stair gate equipment. My personal preference is to attach wooden gates that screw into the wall or stair-case. Not only does this mean that you use the stair gate at all times, you avoid the very real danger of erecting a temporary stair gate which can be pushed over, or pulled on to your baby if fitted incorrectly.

- Fix safety catches on washing machine and tumbledryer doors as well as on cupboards in the kitchen and dining room. Although some parents find that, at first, the child-proof locks are a nuisance, they soon adapt to having to use them. Otherwise you may find that you spend a lot of time attempting to dissuade your baby from pulling out crockery or pans. In addition, there is the very real risk of injury to little fingers, since having learnt to open the cupboards your baby will soon also enjoy slamming them shut.

- Fasten polystyrene protectors on the top of the doors. This will ensure that little fingers are protected from slams.

TOP TIP
Spend some time crawling along the floor yourself. This will give you an impression of your home from your baby's viewpoint. You will develop a better awareness of the temptations and attractions to little fingers.

- Re-organise objects to ensure that they are out of reach. This might involve storing wellington boots in the car, or making a new key shelf. You can guarantee that your baby will always pick up and chew the one thing that you least want him to.

- Find new homes for any kitchen or bathroom cleaners, dishwasher tablets, boxes of washing powder, etc. to ensure that these are out of reach.

- Have a strict policy on matches and candles. Never put them where a child could reach. If you use an open fire, make sure you have an effective fireguard.

- The Fire Brigade offer a free service whereby they will come and assess your house for fire risks. They can advise on safety in the kitchen, and will encourage you to fit appropriate alarms, as well as fire extinguishers and fire blankets.

- Remove all wires from the reach of your baby or ensure that they are fastened to walls or skirting boards. If your baby pulls a lamp on top of himself it could lead to a nasty injury.

- Be aware that cooking with a young baby crawling on the floor can be dangerous. Always place your baby a good distance away from the stove or oven. Remember that if you were to drop a pan or kettle it could bounce towards where your baby is seated.

- Keep the handles of any saucepan you are using turned inwards, so that your baby could not reach up and pull a pan down on himself.

- If you can, try to cook on the back rings of your hob. This can protect your baby from spilt pans.

- Never drink a hot drink while holding your baby, and be aware that it is easy to spill a drink if you were to trip on your crawling child.

- Avoid using tablecloths. Your baby will love pulling at these, and could easily bring down the entire contents of the table, including any hot drinks that are on it.

- Remove household plants from reach and put them on a shelf or windowsill at a safe distance. Some can be toxic if eaten, and even the less poisonous plants can irritate sensitive little fingers when pulled apart.

- Keep all plastic bags out of the way. Invest in a bag tidier and keep this out of reach.

- Ensure that all medicines are safely locked away in a medicine cabinet.

- Ensure that bookshelves and heavy freestanding cupboards are fastened to the wall.

- Soften the corners of sharp-edged coffee tables or chests of drawers with a piece of cloth or ready-made plastic corners.

- Block up your plug sockets with plastic protectors to prevent your baby sticking his fingers in them.

- Buy a carbon monoxide alarm and fit this near the boiler.

- Keep your rubbish bin out of reach.

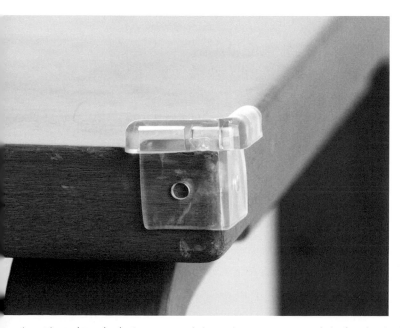

Invest in ready-made plastic corners and plug sockets to prevent your baby from hurting himself

Q&A

Q

I had to go back to work when my son was five months old. He is almost seven months now. His grandparents agreed, very kindly, to look after him until he goes to a childminder in the summer. When they first looked after him he was going through a very bad week due to teething/injections. I tried to explain our routines, and even wrote them out, but, at the time, I could not demonstrate them. I clearly owe a big debt of gratitude to his grandparents, so I do not feel that I can lay down strict rules, however, all my attempts to persuade them to follow our routines have, I think, largely failed. I keep being told that my son is just a baby who will find his own routines in time. After numerous arguments with my husband on the issue, and after accidentally upsetting the grandparents, I now feel that I cannot say anything, so have to bite my tongue when my son sleeps after 5pm or hardly sleeps during the day because 'that was all he wanted'. At present I am beginning to wean him so would like his food to be given to him at the right times of day but don't quite know how to approach this.

Luckily, when I am home, my son

follows the routine again quite well. However, I still can't help being concerned that he may become confused from the mixed messages.

Is there a good way to persuade relatives and, in the future, a child-minder, to follow a routine? If not, are the mixed messages likely to cause a problem?

A

While your son is being cared for by relatives and you know that you need them to help you out, it is probably better to try to tread a

middle path over his daily routine. Although you can write out a routine, it may not always go to plan, especially if he doesn't find it easy to settle to sleep alone in the day. Continue to follow the routine during the days you are at home and hopefully they will begin to see the benefits of having a well-rested baby. Work on areas such as settling him back to sleep, should he wake at lunchtime when you are with him.

The things you could be more specific on are the timings of his

changes to baby's routine

feeds and what he is given to eat in terms of solid food. Prepare the week's menu the weekend before and write it out for your relatives. Before leaving for work, place the meals for the day in the fridge, labelled as to what time they are to be given. Explain as fully as you can why you want your son to be fed this way and how important it is to get his nutritional needs of solids and milk feeds balanced during the day. Again, until the summer, you may have to be a little flexible on this. As a temporary measure, your baby should be able to adapt to the two ways he is cared for as long as you keep the routines up when you are at home. If you feel that the mixed messages are affecting him, sit down with both your husband and relatives and discuss the matter as calmly as possible.

If you have already found your childminder, arrange to see her for a chat about your preferences regarding your son. It will be much easier for you to tell her how you would like his day to be, as the relationship you have with her is quite different to the one you have with your relatives. Unless she is involved with taking and collecting older children from playgroup or school, she should be able to keep

to his usual routine. The two main areas you can insist on are: nap times and feeding. Again, you may need to prepare food at the weekend so you know he will be given what you want him to have, but it is worth the extra work for you to know his needs are being met.

Babies do adapt to being cared for by other carers whose ways may not always be the same as your own. Given that you remain consistent with him and keep in close touch with your childminder once he begins there, you will find he should remain pretty content with his daily routine even if there are a few minor differences.

Q

My seven-month-old daughter has learnt to roll on to her front but she cannot get back again and so wakes up several times a night screaming. How can I prevent this happening?

A

Until your daughter learns to roll both ways with ease you may have to go into her room at night and help her turn on to her back. If you have not already started to use a sleeping bag, it is advisable to do so once your baby is moving

around at night. At this stage it is important to get the correct tog for the time of year, you should be able to take away all blankets or sheets you may have used for coverings. This will prevent the problem of your daughter becoming tangled in the bedding or waking through being cold, having kicked off her blankets.

To encourage her to learn to roll both ways without needing your help, practise rolling backwards and forwards with her as much as possible in the daytime.

Once you feel that she is able to roll both ways without your help, leave her for a short while if she wakes in the night to see if she is able to settle herself. If you always go straight to her whenever she wakes, she may begin to associate falling asleep with you being there.

Once she does roll both ways with confidence, allow her to find her own sleeping position. You could try putting her down on her tummy for some of her daytime naps. Some babies come to prefer sleeping in this position when they are able to roll well.

The Eighth Month

PHYSICALLY YOUR BABY IS DEVELOPING QUICKLY. HE MAY BE VERY active, perhaps crawling, or showing a desire to crawl by trying to push himself up on his arms and legs when lying on his tummy. He may also be attempting to hold on to furniture in a bid to pull himself up. If your baby shows no signs of wanting to crawl, there is no cause for concern. Some babies bypass this stage completely and will progress directly to walking in their own time.

It is inevitable that your baby will catch a cold at some point during his first year. This can often happen around this age, as your baby starts to socialise more and may attend regular playgroups or nursery. Although colds are not serious, because young babies cannot blow their own noses, a blocked nose can lead to difficulty in breathing, particularly at night. Getting up in the night to tend to a distressed baby can be very tiring, but as colds usually run their course over five to ten days, this should only be a temporary state of affairs.

Dealing with colds

A cold often leads to a baby refusing solid food, or eating very little. If this happens you may have to go back to offering him milk in the night until he is better. When a young baby is ill, it is important that he is not allowed to become dehydrated. Do not worry that by giving him milk in the night it will become a habit. Once he has fully recovered you can easily get rid of any middle-of-the-night milk feeds once his intake of solids increases.

> **INFECTIONS**
> If your baby develops a fever, suffers from persistent chestiness and coughing, or the mucus from his nose takes on a green colour, it would be advisable to have him checked by the doctor to ensure that the cold has not developed into an infection.

- You will probably find that your baby gets more distressed after he has been lying flat for any length of time. During a cold it often helps to have the mattress slightly elevated on a slope. It is also advisable to put a draw sheet – a smaller sheet lying across the mattress and underneath the baby – across the cot so that you do not have to change the whole sheet should it become wet from his runny nose.

- A small suction bulb can be bought from your pharmacy that is specially designed to help clear babies' noses and you might find that this helps. Alternatively you could try using one of the electic oil vaporisers that diffuses vapour into his room which helps clear his breathing passages. These are particularly effective at night.

- It is obviously very upsetting to see your baby unwell and in discomfort, but try to sound positive and reassuring when comforting him. He will sense it if you sound panicky and that will only make him more upset.

Feeding

Your baby will continue to need three milk feeds and three solid meals a day. If he is happily taking small amounts of other fluids from his beaker, you should try giving him his 2.30pm milk from a beaker too.

Solids

- This month it is important to start increasing the amount of finger foods, finely chopped and diced food your baby is eating, while decreasing the amount of puréed and mashed or pulsed food. Meat, chicken and fish should still be pulsed, however.

- Experiment with different finger foods, more of which should be going into his mouth now, rather than being squeezed or played with.

- Always try to eat breakfast at the same time as your baby, and if you have managed to move his lunch onto 12 noon, then eating with him at this time will also help him develop good eating habits and table manners.

- Babies love to copy and imitate adults, so encouraging him to use a spoon, and later, a fork, will be more successful if he has the opportunity to see you doing it.

- Your baby should now be enjoying a proper tea at 5pm. This could consist of mini-sandwiches, baked potato or small pasta shapes served with sauce and vegetables. Do not allow too large a drink with this meal, as it will put him off his later milk feed. However, if your baby becomes very tired and fussy around this time, and if he has eaten well at his other meals, you could offer him a milk pudding, cereal or a yoghurt instead of a full tea.

A visual feast

The appearance of your baby's meals becomes very important at this age and foods should not be mashed up and mixed together at this stage. Try to arrange the food attractively on his plate with a variety of different-coloured

> ### SHARING THE CARE
> If your baby catches a cold you will more than likely have to attend to him at least once in the night and perhaps even more often. If you are back at work, getting up in the night can be exhausting. It is a good idea if you and your husband split the care of the baby in the night. If one of you takes sole charge from, say, 9pm to 1am, the other one can go to bed early to get some uninterrupted sleep, before taking over at 1am. Then you will both at least have had a few hours of uninterrupted sleep, which makes more sense than you both being woken up several times a night.

vegetables or fruit as babies are very aware of texture and colour. However, do not overload his plate or bowl; serve up a small amount and when he has finished that, replenish his plate. This helps avoid the game of throwing the food on the floor, which can start at this stage.

Encouraging self-feeding

When feeding your baby use two spoons, and allow him to hold one to try and scoop up some of the food for himself. Holding his wrist and gently helping him manoeuvre the spoon to his mouth will encourage him to take an interest in self-feeding.

You will still need to spoon-feed him most of his solids at this stage, but it is worthwhile spending a little time at each meal helping him practise with the spoon.

Helping your baby hold his spoon will encourage him to try to feed himself

Sleeping

- Babies of eight to nine months of age need approximately two and a half to three hours sleep between the hours of 7am and 7pm. This is usually divided between one short nap in the morning and one longer nap after lunch.

- Some babies that are sleeping 12 hours at night may start to cut back on their daytime sleep. If you notice that your baby is cutting right back on his lunchtime nap, it would be advisable to allow him only a very short nap in the morning so that he sleeps well at lunchtime.

- Cutting back the lunchtime nap is particularly important if you are a working mother who wants her baby to stay up later in the evening. He will be unlikely to do this if he has only had a short nap after lunch.

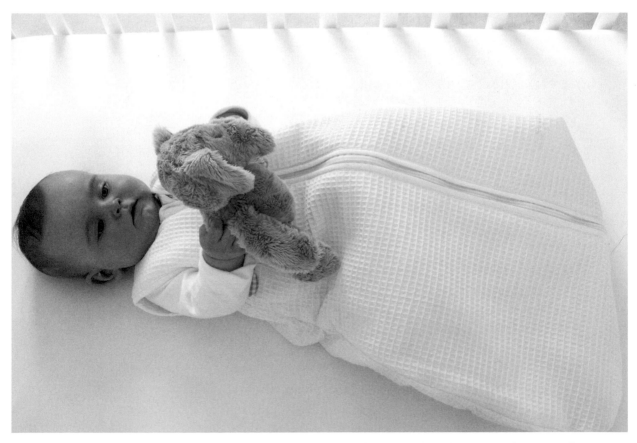

Once the bedding has been removed from the cot some babies miss the security of being tucked in and you may need to put a small comforter in the cot to help settle your baby

The bed and bathtime routine

SAFETY IN THE BATH
At bathtime, always use a long non-slip mat in the bath and, if needed, place a tap protector over any hot taps that your baby is close to. To prevent accidents, never let him stand up in the bath. If he protests at having to sit down, then end bathtime. He may protest, but slipping in the bath can cause nasty bumps and bangs as well as the danger of chipped teeth, slipping under the water and generally becoming fearful of water.

- Continue with your established bedtime routine.

- You may find that during this month your baby will start to sit up in his cot, but will not get himself back down again, and you may end up having to go in several times a night to lay him back down to sleep.

- It is a good idea, when settling your baby in his cot at sleep times, to start putting him in the cot in a sitting position, instead of laying him down on his side or back. Then encourage him to lay himself down. This will help him to do the same when he wakes in the night.

Development

Mental development

During this month your baby will begin to understand that he is a separate person from you. This can lead to him becoming clingier. He may demand more of your attention, as he wants to stay as close to you as possible, knowing that you can disappear. He will be more wary of strangers and may not want to be left with unfamiliar people. In a crowded place he will cling tightly to you.

- Your baby will be aware of all the close members of his family. He will recognise them from photos and become excited by faces in mirrors. If he does not already have a photo album for himself, make him one that

Your baby's vocal sounds are becoming
more varied and you will probably
know what he is trying to tell you by
his noises and facial expressions

includes pictures of people he may not see so often, such as grandparents, to
help him remember who they are.

- Your baby's vocal sounds are becoming more varied and you will probably
know what he is trying to tell you by his noises and facial expressions. He
will try to copy the sounds that you make and will repeat sounds over and
over again. He is able to understand 'Yes' and 'No', especially if accompanied with a smiling or firm face. Try to limit the 'No's to things which are
really important.

- He may learn to point using his index finger. This can help him to let you
know what he wants, despite his lack of language.

- He will be able to tell the difference between 'Mummy's hat' and 'Baby's
hat', which you can see by watching the expression on his face when you
ask him to whom the hat belongs.

Physical development

Physically your baby is developing quickly. Some babies may now be able to
crawl, both forwards and backwards, or may have found another way to move
around. If you have wooden floors your baby may have developed 'bottom
shuffling', as this is easier on a smooth surface. Even if he is not mobile your
baby will be sitting well and should be able to rock himself forwards and
backwards to help him get to a toy just out of reach.

- Your baby will find lots of uses for his toys now. He will be able to play
with two or more objects at once, such as putting small blocks into nesting
cups, pouring and emptying cups when in the bath, banging on a drum

with a stick or bricks. He will run his cars and trucks up and down, maybe with one in each hand.

• If held in a standing position against a solid piece of furniture, he will hold on tightly and be delighted in seeing the world from a different height. He will still find it quite hard to pull himself up to a standing position alone, but if given plenty of opportunities to try, he will get better at this. By the end of the month, a few babies are even able to 'cruise' a little, walking with both hands firmly holding on to a piece of furniture to steady themselves.

• By eight months of age, your baby's vision is almost fully developed, although his ability to focus quickly continues to develop during the first year.

SAFETY TIP
Your baby will notice tiny flecks of fluff and crumbs and may try to pick them up, using his developing pincer grasp. This is when you need to be vigilant about leaving small things such as coins, buttons and pins around. Your baby will put most things he finds into his mouth.

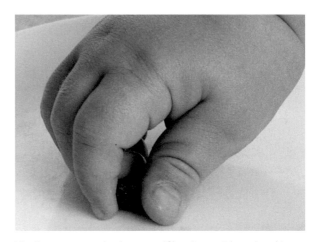

His pincer grasp can be dangerous if he tries to pick up tiny objects

The eight-month check

During the eighth month your GP or nurse will carry out a developmental check on your baby. This is also an opportunity for you to discuss whether you have any concerns regarding your baby's development. The following will be checked:

Weight and length
Your baby will be weighed and measured and the details entered into his health book.

Hearing

This is a basic test involving you or the GP making a sound and carefully watching your baby's response to see if he has heard it. If you are concerned, or if the GP feels there is any reason for a second opinion, you will be offered further tests at hospital at a later date.

Eyesight

Your baby will be observed to see how he looks at objects and checked for any sign of a squint. The GP will see if he can track a moving object around the room.

Sounds

Your GP will ask you what sounds your baby is able to make, as these are an important stepping-stone to speech.

Handling skills

Your baby's developing motor-neurone skills may be also be observed, in which case he will be given a small toy to handle and play with.

Spine and hips

They will be examined to check if there are any development problems. Your baby's hips will be gently rotated to check for any dislocation, or 'clicky hip'.

Genitals

If you have a boy, your baby's testes will be examined to see if they have descended. It is not uncommon for a baby boy to need a straightforward operation to correct this.

Encouraging development through play

- If he is not yet crawling, encourage your baby to roll over and over so he is able to get to things out of reach. This will help him to be less demanding of you. A baby who sits in one place will become bored quickly with the toys he can reach, and will shout for attention.

- Your baby can now open and close his hands voluntarily and will continue to enjoy simple action rhymes and games. Show him how to wave 'Bye, bye',

Encourage your baby's motor skill development by showing him how to wave 'bye, bye'

which he will do by opening and closing his raised hand. He will also delight in dropping toys over and over again, watching to see where they have fallen. If you have not already attached some toys to lengths of ribbon so that he can retrieve them (see page 147), you may want to do so now, as your baby can carry on with this game long after you want to.

Socially your baby will like to be in the company of other babies and small children

- His growing sense of balance and control of his whole body will help him enjoy more physical play such as being held up high, turned upside down and swung safely. This type of play is often enjoyed between fathers and their children. Provided care is taken not to jerk necks backwards and forwards or swing by the arms or legs, most babies will enjoy the sensations of flying, turning upside down and swinging.

- Baby-proofing certain areas so your baby is able to explore safely will help you both. When you do use 'No' try to give a simple explanation such as 'No, we don't touch the oven, it's hot'. He will learn the differences between hot and cold, hard and soft and other contrasts if you use these words often and in their context.

- Now he is familiar with animals through his books introduce your baby to some real ones if you can, especially if you don't have pets of your own. Find a local children's farm or pet's corner to visit. Let him watch the animals for as long as he likes. If he wants to touch them, and it is allowed, then let him but remember to wash his hands thoroughly before you leave.

- Socially your baby will like to be in the company of other babies and small children. Once mobile you may have to watch he does not get too enthusiastic when grabbing at another baby. He does not mean to harm or frighten, he is just exploring. Use distraction as much as possible to prevent over-enthusiastic behaviour and always explain very simply to your baby why he may not hurt others, removing him if necessary. Gradually he will come to understand how to treat other children.

You will need to watch your baby does not get too boisterous when playing with other babies

- Trips to the park will always be enjoyed, especially as your baby can sit up well in a baby swing. He may like being taken down a short slide or gently bounced on a seesaw.

Toys, games and books

- Now that he is more dextrous in his hand movements, introduce building blocks which lock together. There are plenty of sets available which incorporate people, animals, cars and other items to create miniature worlds. Show him how to lock the blocks together but don't always make a whole play set for him. Encourage him to do it for himself. Once he has learnt how to fix the bricks and objects together he will have a toy that will give him plenty of pleasure for a long time.

- He may be able to fit his nesting cups inside each other although the ones very similar in size may baffle him. Keep showing him how to do it and use appropriate language to explain your actions. He will still enjoy knocking down the towers that you build.

- Bathtime will be a popular time of day. Encourage him to fill and empty plastic cups, bottles and small watering cans, and keep using language to reinforce his actions.

Q&A refusing food

Q

My eight-month-old daughter is beginning to refuse to eat her meals without distraction and every meal is taking a long time.

At the end of a 45-minute battle, and with a lot of distraction, I usually manage to get her to finish her meal, but I am very worried that if I continue like this, she will never learn to eat a meal on her own and may even hate eating food as she gets older.

A

Around this age it is not unusual for a baby to start resisting being fed with a spoon. It is easy to become concerned that your baby is not eating enough food and, like many parents, you will try any form of distraction that will encourage eating.

Babies of this age are gaining more independence. They want to do things for themselves and may resist the attempts of adults to feed them. If you insist on feeding your daughter yourself, you may find that she completely refuses to be spoon-fed and becomes increasingly frustra-ted. Letting your baby self-feed can be messy but it is an important part of her development. Let your daughter hold a spoon and show her how to dig into her food. Things

such as mashed potato will stay quite well on a spoon even if she turns it over before it reaches her mouth.

Keep trying different finger foods to tempt her. Tea could consist of small pieces of homemade pizza, quiche or mini sandwiches.

Your daughter is also becoming much more aware and interested in the appearance of her food and will be attracted by colour, shape and texture. Provide her with plenty of variety, e.g. rather than offering just one or two vegetables with her protein at lunch try giving her smaller amounts of three or four vegetables, such as a spoonful of peas, a piece of baby corn, two broccoli florets and some diced carrots.

Be aware of the amounts of food you can realistically expect your daughter to eat at a meal, as you may be over-estimating the size of her portions. For example, a baby's serving of carbohydrates is 25g [1oz] of cereal, two tablespoons of pasta or a slice of bread. It easy to think that as your baby grows she will need bigger portions but towards the end of the first year her growth rate has begun to slow down, so she may not actually need as much food as you think.

It is all too easy to slip into the

habit of giving your daughter sweet foods such as fruit yoghurts and fromage frais when she appears to have eaten little of her savoury course, as you know these will be accepted and at least she will have eaten something. However, a baby of this age will quickly learn that if she makes enough fuss over her first course she will be offered a food she prefers. If your daughter has eaten a small amount of her main course but really doesn't seem interested in more, clear the dishes away and offer some fresh fruit or a stick of cheese instead.

Always make sure that you are offering meals well spaced apart and try moving her lunchtime on to nearer noon. She may also be quite active by now so watch that you are not trying to feed her when she is too tired to eat properly. This can often happen at teatime.

Above all, try to make mealtimes into relaxed and happy occasions, as your daughter will sense any stress or tension from you. If possible, sit down with her yourself to eat at least one meal a day.

The Ninth Month

Y OUR BABY HAS BECOME MORE SOCIABLE AND MAY ENJOY PLAYING TO an audience, especially if he knows he is being watched. He may even begin to repeat certain actions knowing that they make you or other people laugh, revealing his developing sense of humour. Exploring the world around him will be ever-more important and, if your baby is on the move, he will be investigating everything within his reach.

This is a good age to have one last holiday that revolves more round your needs as a couple rather than your baby's. He is at an age where he will still be happy to sit for reasonable periods in his buggy while you trawl around galleries and shopping centres. Next year, when he is a toddler, you will most definitely have to choose somewhere that will meet his needs. He will be running around and will need to be entertained and have the opportunity to mix with other children. Perhaps now is a good time to consider that one last visit to your favourite city in Europe or, if you have always enjoyed outdoor pursuits such as hill-walking or camping, this will still be possible for as long as your baby is happy to sit in a backpack for a couple of hours at a time.

A unique individual

Your baby's individual personality is quite apparent by now and you will have a good idea of his temperament; whether he is shy or sociable, easygoing or challenging, introvert or extrovert. Whatever his personal qualities, over the last few months you will have developed your own ways of dealing with him based on your understanding of his personality and needs. You will know, for example, whether he enjoys 'rough play' or is a child that needs more sensitive handling and you will have unconsciously adapted his daily activities to fit in with his preferences.

No one knows for sure how much of a baby's personality is pre-determined, or inherited, and how much it is influenced by his parents and upbringing. There are parents who can clearly see their own or their spouse's

By now you will have a good idea of
your baby's temperament: take time to
enjoy watching his little personality
grow and develop

characteristics reflected in their baby's temperament and others who are
surprised by how different their children are from themselves. However your
baby's personality is developing, try to focus on the positive strengths that
come with his unique characteristics and take time to enjoy watching his
little personality grow and develop.

Twins

Parents of twin babies will find it even
more fascinating to watch the two of
them develop and to see how similar – or
different – they turn out to be. Research
has found that identical twins (babies who
have grown from a single fertilised egg,
and are therefore the same sex) generally
follow a similar pattern of social
development and are extremely likely to
share the same characteristics, attitudes
and reactions. They are usually very close,
forming their own little 'unit'; some even
speak their own twin 'language'. It has
been found that fraternal twins, however,
(twins who come from two different eggs
fertilised by different sperm) may be as
different from each other as any pair of
siblings.

If you are the parent of twins, detailed
information about their care can be
found in *A Contented House with Twins*.

It is normal for a lot of mess to be created when your baby starts to try and feed himself

Feeding

- Your baby will still be having three milk feeds a day at this age, but you may find that he becomes less interested in his milk and starts to cut back on the amount he takes.

- His morning feed and evening milk feed are still very important, so if he is refusing milk or cutting back at either of these feeds, it would be advisable to reduce his 2.30pm feed, or replace it altogether with a drink of water or well-diluted juice to ensure that he takes a good milk feed at bedtime.

- He still needs a minimum of 530ml (18oz) of formula milk a day, inclusive of milk used in cooking.

- If necessary, you can increase the amount of milk he is taking by giving him more meals with milk-based sauces, or by offering him a milk pudding or yoghurt after lunch or in the evening.

> **TOP TIP**
> Be prepared for the mess that will be generated by your baby trying to feed himself and cover the floor with newspaper or special splash mat under his high chair.

- Apart from his last milk feed of the day, try to encourage your baby to take any other milk he is having from a beaker.

- Continue with a variety of finger foods and finely chop and dice most of his other foods to help him get used to chewing. Meat, chicken and fish may still need to be pulsed, however, depending on how many teeth your baby has.

Messy eating

Your baby may be managing to eat at least some of his meal using his spoon. This may mean that lunchtimes are messier, and take longer, but it is part of him learning to be independent and this should be encouraged. Serving him meals that consist of lots of finger foods, diced, sliced, and chopped foods, as opposed to mashed and pulsed will help reduce the mess. Putting only small amounts of food on his plate at a time, instead of the full meal will also lessen the chance of him playing with the food and throwing it on the floor. If he does start to do this it is important to be quite firm, remove the plate for a few minutes, and tell him in a firm voice, 'No throwing'. When you give him the plate back, if he does the same thing again, you should end the meal and remove him from the high chair. He will learn very quickly that food is for eating and not for playing with.

Sleeping

- At nine months babies usually need approximately two and a half to three hours sleep during the day if they are to sleep for 11–12 hours at night.

- This should be divided up into two separate naps. The lunchtime nap should always be the longer of the two naps.

- If your baby is sleeping until 8am in the morning and you want him to continue going down at 7pm in the evening, you should cut out the morning nap and allow him one long nap after lunch.

- However, if you want your baby to stay up slightly later in the evening, then you should give him a short nap at around 10am, followed by a longer nap at 1pm. This should help him get through until nearer 8pm without becoming overtired.

The bed and bathtime routine

Continue with the established bathtime routine and ensure your baby has his bath at 6pm each day and that he is massaged and dressed and ready for a feed at 6.30pm.

Allow him to sit quietly in his chair with the lights dimmed for a few minutes after his 6.30pm feed, before settling him into his cot.

Development

Mental development

- You may now notice two distinct syllables being put together, such as 'Muh-geh'. The 'Da, da' you may have been hearing for a while will be said more often when his father is in the room, and with more meaning. Your baby will be able increasingly to understand simple instructions such as, 'Come here'.

Your baby is very aware of other children

- Your baby will enjoy simple story lines now, and there are plenty of picture books for the very young around which he will like you to read to him. He will also love looking at the relevant pictures, which you can talk about, pointing out things he recognises such as animals and people.

At this age babies may be quite protective of the toys they are playing with

- He is aware of being watched and may enjoy playing to an audience. He has a sense of fun and his favourite games will probably be emptying and filling things and throwing things down.

- He is very aware of other children and may become upset himself if he sees other babies upset. He will protect the toy he is playing with if he thinks someone is going to take it from him.

Physical development

Between nine and 12 months your baby may be able to walk if his hands are held; some babies may even be able to take several steps unaided.

- Your baby may be becoming more proficient at moving around. Crawling can take several forms. Some babies may prefer a more 'commando' style, where they keep their tummies on the floor and use their arms to pull themselves along. A baby may crawl in this way for a time before getting up on all fours. Others may 'bear walk', where the knees are kept off the ground completely. This may happen if a baby spends time outside on grass, or does not like crawling with bare knees on sisal-type carpets.

Encouraging development through play

- Whichever way your baby decides he wants to move, encourage him.

- Place toys in a trail for him to find, roll balls in front of him or slowly pull a wheeled toy so he can follow.

- Once he crawls well he may enjoy having an obstacle course set up. You can buy play tunnels and cubes which encourage crawling, or make your own using large cardboard boxes with both ends opened, blankets thrown over low tables and large floor cushions placed in line to crawl over.

- Encourage him to stand holding on to firm chairs and other sturdy pieces of furniture. Place a toy beyond his reach and see if he will begin to 'side-step' towards it. Babies can cruise around the furniture happily once they feel secure. They will drop on to all fours when the hand holds run out and then crawl to the next piece of furniture to pull themselves up on.

- You may like to arrange your furniture to encourage cruising.

Toys, games and books

- Try reading your baby some of the many lift-the-flap books on the market. These will provide plenty of fun and anticipation and he may even tear the flaps in his enthusiasm to see what is underneath. Try to mend the books as soon as you can. Wear and tear is inevitable with books that are used often but by always patching and mending them as soon as possible, your baby will begin to learn that books need to be looked after.

- There are also soft 'busy' books available which have different activities on each page, such as zips, buttons, Velcro fastening, laces, etc. Obviously, some actions will still be beyond his skills, but he may enjoy tackling the easier ones.

SAFETY TIP

Many babies do not crawl at all; some become proficient at bottom shuffling then pull themselves to standing, others find different ways of becoming mobile to explore their surroundings.

Depending on how inquisitive your baby is you may need to put cupboard locks on every door or else move fragile or dangerous items such as cleaning materials to higher cupboards. See page 163 for more detailed safety guidelines.

Some people will baby-proof every cupboard door, however, teaching your baby that there are some things he may not touch will help you in other people's houses. He needs to learn that he cannot have everything he sees. But do make sure that there is nothing dangerous left in any unlocked cupboards.

- Let him have simple board books in an accessible place close to his toys. Clear a space for him on the bottom of your shelves to keep his books on. Emptying shelves is a favourite pastime at this age so by removing your own books and replacing them with your baby's, he will be able to empty a shelf with no real damage caused.

- Incorporate plenty of nursery rhymes into your reading sessions, as well as throughout the day, to encourage both his sense of rhythm and language acquisition. Find one or two collections that contain all your favourites. He may well anticipate the words of well-known rhymes and make attempts to finish the last word of a line if you pause for a short while.

> ### ENCOURAGING SPEECH
> As you talk to your baby, telling him what you are doing, what he is doing, what you can see and talking him through all the daily tasks, such as dressing and getting ready for a meal, he will begin to link words with objects and actions and try to copy you.

- Continue to supplement your baby's toys with household articles. Since he loves to empty and fill things, find a low drawer or cupboard in the kitchen which can become 'his'. Use plastic pots and boxes with lids, cardboard tubes, paper bags, plastic utensils, wooden spoons, plastic bowls, bread baskets and any other items such as his beakers and bowls. While you are busy in the kitchen he will be able to take things out and put them back without doing any harm. Should he begin to open your cupboards and drawers, explain to him that they are Mummy's and he must play with his own.

- Toys he will now enjoy are those which are replicas of real things he sees around him. A toy phone will be used with amazing accuracy; you will see how much he has taken in watching you over the past few months. He may also enjoy a simple plastic tea set. Watch to see if he offers his teddies a drink, having watched you do so. He will know that a brush is for his hair, whether it is his own hairbrush or the floor brush left within his reach.

- Find pop-up toys, which need his forefinger to operate them. He will love anything with buttons to push, bells to ring and dials to turn, especially if rewarded with an object popping up. There are small 'pop-up men' in a wooden block that will pop up when pushed. This simple toy may keep him amused for as long as a more complicated one with lots of lights and noise.

- Show him how to build a small tower with two blocks. By the end of this month he may have managed to do this by himself as he can now let go and judge distances better.

- If he is quite steady when standing, he may enjoy a sturdy push-along truck. Check that it won't tip over when leant on too hard. You may need to be there with a steadying hand until he learns more control and doesn't push too hard.

- Your baby will be aware of textures such as smooth, wet, soft or hard surfaces. Try to provide him with opportunities to explore the properties of both water and dry sand. Protect the floor and let him have a small bowl of warm water to dabble in. Provide small cups, plastic scoops, spoons, sieves

Babies of this age are often fascinated by objects they have seen you use such as mobile phones

Help your baby to try and build towers with blocks. It won't be long before he will be able to build them on his own

and other items that will float. Colour the water with food dye for a change or add a squirt of baby bath to produce bubbles. Keep a tub of bubbles handy to blow when he has had a bad fall, lunch is late or at any other time of day when you need to distract him.

- Dry sand suitable for children can be bought at a good toyshop. A small bag can be used in a washing-up bowl and a few toys added. Your baby will enjoy the feeling of sand running over his fingers and will be absorbed by filling and emptying small plastic pots. He may attempt to put sand in his mouth but if you are firm about this and distract him by showing him something new he will soon stop. Don't allow him to throw sand. If he won't stop, remove him or put the bowl away for another day.

Q & A

pets

Q

We have just moved to a house in the countryside. Our neighbours have offered us a puppy from their forthcoming litter. We are very tempted to take the puppy since I would love a dog, and we want our son to grow up with a pet. Our son Tom is nine months now and is a happy contented baby. He is just starting to crawl and we have 'baby-proofed' the areas where he is allowed to roam. Are we taking on too much to consider having a puppy in the house and what are the problems we might face?

A

Having a puppy in the house is not impossible, but you will need to think carefully about how you will cope.

Deciding where the puppy will and will not be allowed is the first consideration. If your kitchen is large and has access to an outside area, then keep the puppy mainly there, at least until he is house trained.

Consider where the dog's bed will be, and keep this place strictly off-limits to Tom at all times. Think how you can restrict the puppy to a smallish area overnight while house training him. Who will be the one to clear up in the morning?

Tom may well be clamouring for breakfast when the kitchen floor is awash with soiled newspaper.

Consider where you will feed the dog and also where he can have access to a water bowl. Both places must be off limits to Tom and he must be taught not to go near the dog when he is eating or drinking. Keep all feeding bowls scrupulously clean. Putting them down on old newspapers greatly helps in clearing up after each feed.

At this age Tom will put everything he finds into his mouth so the floor must be kept well swept and washed daily. Be aware that Tom will not know the difference between his toys and the puppy's, so could pick up the puppy's toys off the floor and put them in his mouth. Equally the puppy will not know the difference between his toys and Tom's, and could well chew up rattles and bricks if they are left on the floor.

On a practical note, wipe Tom's toys over every few days with a mild disinfectant or anti-bacterial cleaner, in case they have been licked by the puppy.

Using stair gates to close off areas can work well in a kitchen. Tom will not want to be 'penned in' too much, but at times you may not want both puppy and baby together and under your feet at the same time.

Tom will need to be taught that the puppy is not just another toy and that he may not pull or grab his tail or ears. The puppy will also need to be taught that he may not nip, even in play.

Teaching Tom to have respect for all animals is another valuable lesson. When babies are brought up alongside puppies they are often unaware that other dogs may not be as tolerant as their own, and they need to be watched near unknown animals.

Just like babies, puppies thrive on routine, so think how you will manage on a day-to-day basis with them both. If you decide to go ahead and take the puppy when he is ready to leave his mother, be prepared for a few frantic weeks. But the pleasure that a family pet can bring to you all will be worth the hard work that comes at the beginning.

The Tenth Month

AT TEN MONTHS YOUR BABY IS ABLE TO EXPRESS HIS AFFECTION FOR you with more and more demonstrative actions. He may snuggle into you when you are sharing a book or a quiet moment together and begin to cuddle and kiss you. If he wants your attention he will pull at you until he gets it. He is showing that he has a mind of his own and this becomes quite apparent when he is objecting to something he doesn't like. If he's not in the mood for wearing a hat on a certain day, or being strapped into his buggy, you will certainly know about it.

As he becomes more mobile, you'll be spending much of your time following him around, especially when in unfamiliar places. Keeping an eye on an active baby can be a demanding job and you will probably find that both you and your baby are very tired at the end of the day.

This month is an ideal stage for dads to start having some time alone with their baby if they're not already doing so and it will also allow Mum to have some time to herself for a bit of pampering. Babies can be fascinated by even the most mundane of chores and outings, such as a visit to the supermarket or the tip, but you could also do something that is relaxing for you such as a walk in the park to feed the ducks.

Siblings and the age gap

Child psychologists suggest that the optimum gap between siblings is 18 months to two and a half years. Numerous factors may determine the age gap that you have between your children.

- Some parents prefer to coincide the arrival of their second child with their first child's introduction to nursery school. This can work very well, since by two and a half, your elder child is developing an independent social life and is less likely to be jealous of the new baby. It will, however, be longer before they are able to play together.

- The attractions of a small gap are undoubtedly the children's compatibility in play as they grow up.

TWO UNDER TWO

Having two children under the age of two is hard work. It will probably involve double nappy changes for a period. You will be experiencing toddler milestones, such as the transition from cot to bed and potty training, while juggling the demands of a new baby. There will be two very dependent little people both requiring a great deal of care, and probably still at home 24 hours a day. The benefits are that your children will have plenty of time to bond with each other. Your new baby will love the noise, fun and attention provided by the older child at home. Your toddler will offer endless entertainment, although you will need to closely monitor his attentions to the newborn baby.

- If you are an older mother you will probably be keen to complete your family.

- The age gap that occurs between siblings, whether by design or Mother Nature, will no doubt suit your family in the long run.

Feeding

- Your baby will need two to three milk feeds per day.

- Between nine and 12 months many babies cut out their 2.30pm milk. If your baby has done this and you are worried that his milk intake is too low, try giving him meals like pasta and vegetables with a milk sauce, baked potatoes with grated cheese, mini quiches, or a yoghurt for pudding.

- Your baby will love to use his hands so let him feed himself as much as possible.

- He may still need help with his spoon, especially with runnier foods, but he should be able to self-feed most of his meal.

- Putting his food into a deep bowl or beaker rather than on a plate will make it easier for him to scoop it up.

> **TOP TIP**
> Remember that your baby still does not know the difference between thirst and hunger, and allowing him to drink excessive amounts of fluids in between meals could take the edge off his appetite. Try to allow two hours in between snack and drinks, and mealtimes.

- Continue to finely chop or dice your baby's food rather than mashing it as it is important that your baby learns to chew properly. Meat will still need to be pulsed or very finely chopped.

Food refusal

Your baby should be enjoying a wide variety of foods now, but you may find that his appetite varies considerably from one meal to the next, or from one day to the next. It is really important that you do not get into the habit of cajoling him to eat. He will eat when he is hungry, and you may find that there are days when he will refuse most of the food offered to him. This can be worrying and you may be tempted to offer him lots of alternatives, just so you know that he has had something. This is not really advisable, as it usually leads babies to become even fussier. Try keeping a food diary for several days of everything he eats and drinks, to see if there is a pattern to his food refusal. Often it can happen on days when he has had a very busy morning, or days when he has been at playgroup or nursery and has been offered a drink or biscuit too near lunchtime.

Drinks

Formula-fed babies should be having all their milk drinks from a beaker now, apart from his last bedtime milk. A drink of well-diluted pure unsweetened fruit juice in a beaker will help the absorption of iron at lunchtime, but make sure your baby has most of his meal before you allow him to finish the drink.

Sleeping

- Babies of 10 months of age need approximately two and a half to three hours sleep between the hours of 7am and 7pm or 8am and 8pm.

- This should be divided up into two separate naps, or for a baby sleeping 8am to 8pm, one long nap after lunch.

- To avoid overtiredness and early-morning waking, try to structure your baby's naps so that he has a shorter nap in the morning and a longer nap after lunch.

- Your baby might also start to pull

himself up in his cot at this stage and may not be able to get down again without some help, which means you may have to get up in the night and help put him back down to sleep. To prevent this becoming a habit, encourage him to practise getting up and down by himself.

- When you put him in the cot at sleep times, put him in standing up, then encourage him to put his hands on the bars. With your hands, help him to lower himself down to a sleeping position with his hands holding on to the bars.

A drink of well-diluted pure unsweetened fruit juice in a beaker will help your baby's absorption of iron at lunchtime

Encouraging your baby to get up and down in his cot by himself should prevent you having to get up in the night to help him if he gets stuck

The bed and bathtime routine

Continue with the established bathtime routine and ensure your baby has his bath at 6pm each day and that he is massaged and dressed and ready for a feed at 6.30pm.

Allow him to sit quietly in his cot with the lights dimmed for a few minutes before encouraging him to settle himself into the lying position (see page 201).

Development

Mental development

Although your baby will still be mouthing his toys, as his fine finger and hand skills have improved he can find out a great deal without having to use his mouth. But with smaller objects such as stones, coins and buttons, the temptation to put them into his mouth is still very strong.

- In between his babbling you may be able to distinguish one or two words, and he is now linking the sounds he makes with the objects he knows. For example, when he sees a dog, either a picture or the real thing, he may say 'da'. As well as the babbling he may chatter constantly. This stream of sounds is his way of copying long conversations he hears from adults. Answering his observations with, 'Oh yes, that's a big dog!' will help him enjoy the social side of conversation-making even though he cannot properly take part in it.

> He will now stop what he is doing and listen if you say his name

- He will now stop what he is doing and listen if you say his name. By using his name a lot during conversation (e.g. 'Where are Jonathan's socks?') you will help him to understand that he is his own person.

- He can also follow simple directions such as, 'Find the teddy. Can Jonathan find the teddy?'

- Your baby now will spend quite a bit of time just observing the world. To help him recognise people and places and remember them point things out for him: 'There's the red bus; there's the school', etc. Asking him, 'Where's the red bus?' the next time you pass one will help improve his recognition.

- He enjoys small toys and will play with simple play figures, cars and plastic animals for longer periods of time. He can now remember a toy and look for it if it is out of sight, although he will soon give up looking when his attention is caught by something else.

- Your baby will try to copy some of your actions. If you give him a cloth he will try to wipe his high chair tray. He will also begin to match things together, such as bowl and spoon or a cup and saucer.

LOUD NOISES

He may suddenly start to have fears of loud noises such as the vacuum cleaner or food mixer. This is usually because he has been startled by them being switched on. To lessen his fear, always tell him before you turn on a noisy appliance. Tell him that everything is all right but there will be a big noise. He may still be upset, so reassure him as much as you can.

- When you are getting him dressed or undressed, encourage your baby to participate by asking him to lift his foot up ready for a sock, hold his arm out for the sleeve of his coat or take the toe of his sock to pull if off. Praise him for his efforts.

- He is still curious about other children but his empathy is not fully developed and he cannot understand that his actions may upset them.

- His separation anxiety may still be apparent and he could be anxious when in new or strange situations. Reassure him with your voice and stay close to him. The tone of your voice is so important as he will pick up any tension or stress from you and become upset.

- Socially he will like to be part of the family. Have as many meals together as you can. He will enjoy being part of the occasion and may draw attention to himself by banging his spoon or bowl. He may like to wave goodbye to Mummy or Daddy in the morning and greet them in the evening.

Physical development

- Physically your baby is developing fast. He can probably crawl at some speed and may even be able to cruise with more confidence now.

- Try not to compare your child with others of a similar age as all babies develop at their own rate.

- If you are concerned about your baby's progress, do talk to your GP or health visitor.

- His pincer grasp is developing well and his fingers are becoming more agile. You may notice his hand preference beginning to show although this is not really fully apparent until well into the second year.

STEPS AND STAIRS
Your baby may have discovered steps or stairs. He may manage one easily but a whole flight is still quite a daunting prospect for him. He will learn to climb up them before learning to come down. Use stair gates where needed but having one or two steps to practise on at times will help him perfect this skill. You can teach him to come down backwards, which is the safest way. Many young children work out a way of slowly sliding down stairs on their tummies. Remember always to supervise your baby near stairs that do not have stair gates attached to them.

Low furniture such as your sofa is ideal for encouraging your baby to cruise

Babies love rifling in their own treasure basket; household objects can be particularly appealing

Encouraging development through play

Encourage your baby's natural inquisitiveness as much as possible.

- Give him old cereal and packing boxes, provided they have no sharp edges or staples. He will also delight in playing with cardboard tubes. Show him how to roll a ping-pong ball down the tube and watch it disappear, then reappear.

- Continue to show him how to build a tower and encourage his efforts. He may find the lockable construction bricks easier especially if you lay out two or three for him to handle.

- He will still enjoy action rhymes a great deal and will now be able to join in with some of the actions such as clapping in 'Pat-a-cake', tickling in 'Round and round the garden' and holding your hands for 'Row, row, row the boat'. Show him how to make his hands go round and round for 'The wheels on the bus'. He may not be able to coordinate his hands well enough

Continue to praise his developing speech

yet but he will enjoy trying to copy you. Sing 'Tommy thumb' to him and point to his fingers as well as holding up your own when singing.

- Continue to praise his developing speech by repeating his words back to him and adding descriptive words such as 'big', 'small' or 'red'. If he says, 'dog' you could reply with, 'Yes, that's a big dog' and emphasise the missing ending so he hears the 'g' sound.

- He will enjoy trips out to feed the ducks in the park and going into different shops, especially if you speak to him about what you are doing.

> **TOP TIP**
> Draw your baby's attention to things but make sure he is able to see from his position in the buggy by crouching down next to him and checking his line of vision.

Toys, games and books

There will be plenty of household items to keep your baby amused now.

- Make him a collection of interesting household playthings. Keep egg boxes and old spice containers, if made from plastic. Your baby will love to fill and empty containers of all shapes and sizes using small toys, bricks and plastic cotton reels. He will also like trying to fit them inside each other.

- You may like to make him a treasure basket that he has out at certain times in the day. This is a basket full of items which are natural. Many babies and children have plenty of plastic toys, and perhaps a few wooden ones, but there are many other textures that they are not aware of. A basket such as this is best played with when you are able to sit with your baby as he may try to suck on some of the objects as part of his exploration of their properties. Different textures such as stone will appeal to him and he may well lick at it. You could also include sponges, wooden napkin rings or soft brushes. Provided you have checked things over for sharp edges or points, and that any stones or shells have been cleaned, let him explore as much as he likes. The idea is that you change the contents of the basket frequently, making sure that you include as much variety of texture as you can.

- To help your baby's growing awareness of matching, find a simple shape-sorter. One which has just three different shapes, such as a circle, square and triangle, will be within his scope. Let him explore it and see if he works out for himself where the shapes need to go. You may need to show him how to open it once or twice so he can reclaim the shapes but then let him have a good try on his own. Only help if he gets really frustrated.

- He may enjoy a busy book or dressing toy which has many different fastenings. Again, he will be able to manage some but not others. Zips may be easy, as are Velcro fastenings. If he likes zips, find him an old handbag or wallet and put in one or two things such as old train passes and a set of keys. It is something else he can fill and empty.

He will enjoy trying to fit objects inside one another

Q&A

clingy baby

Q

I wonder if there is any advice you could give to help my baby from being whingey and clingy. He hangs on to my legs if I am washing up, etc. and wants to be picked up most of the time. He is very active and enjoys being around his older brother and going to play centres. But when we are at home he just wants my constant attention, whether there is anyone around or not. Have you any tips?

A

At this stage in your son's development he will become very interested in you, his primary carer. As he has become more mobile and can explore his surroundings, he needs you to share his discoveries and help him understand the world he sees. It can be a time of frustration for your son as he is desperate to find out how things work but his skills are not always advanced enough for him to manage on his own. As he is acquiring these skills his behaviour may be clingy, especially towards you, whom he views as the centre of his world. You are the one who can help him progress and manage these tasks he so dearly wants to accomplish.

It is fine not to know why your son is behaving in this way but what can you do to help this phase pass? It may be time to go through the toy box and remove those toys which he has now grown out of. Find him simple posting boxes, tray puzzles and Duplo building bricks as well as wooden blocks; toys which incorporate several actions to gain a result. Providing toys that are within your son's comprehension is important. Just as he will be bored with toys that are too young for him, he will quickly lose interest in those which are too advanced.

However, your son will still prefer your company to anything else and the more you interact with him, even just by talking, the quicker he will be able to pass through this phase. If you are washing up, sit him up in his high chair near to you so he can actually see what you are doing instead of just hearing the tantalising splashing sounds coming from above his head.

At this age it may help if you designate one low drawer in the kitchen as his. Fill it with small plastic containers, wooden spoons and other utensils, provided they have no sharp bits. If you are cooking and he wants to be with you, encourage him to explore in his drawer as you stand beside him.

Getting your son to play for short periods alone is also possible. The best way to get him to do this is to play alongside him for a short while. Let him take the lead and find out for himself how his toys work but be there to encourage and help him if he needs it. Once you have been beside him for a while, move to a chair or sofa near to him. Work on getting him to play alone for slightly longer periods every day or so. If he manages five minutes the first day, then try to increase it to seven or eight the next day. Asking him to wait for a few moments before he gets your attention is fine, and should be encouraged, but be realistic as to how long at this age he is able to wait. He lives in the 'here and now' and has no concept of time.

It's quite normal for babies of this age to get upset when you leave the room so rather than cause him any distress, scoop him up and take him with you. You can try and include him in what you need to do such as giving him a duster to play with if you're doing the housework, for example. As with most childhood problems being clingy is a phase babies go through that in time will pass.

The Eleventh Month

HE MAY START TO BE MORE INTERESTED IN OTHER BABIES AND WILL enjoy watching them play. You might like to start making short trips to a soft play area, provided it has a separate section for babies under about 18 months. Try to go when it is not too busy with older, louder children, at least until he is used to it, as they can be very noisy places. Join in with his fun and show him how to crawl through tunnels or over cubes. Some play areas have 'ball ponds' which can provide lots of opportunities for ball-rolling games. Remember, though, that your baby will soon become tired so don't make your visits too long otherwise they may end in tears.

Your baby is now making his wishes very clearly known and you may notice he will change from one mood to another very quickly. If he is stopped from doing something he wants, he may become cross and angry, but by now you will have learnt that he can often be persuaded back into a good mood through distractions such as toys, singing or simply pointing out an interesting sight.

The extended family

With more and more families living farther apart from each other, the role of the grandparents and extended family has changed enormously over the last few years.

As your baby is nearing his first birthday, it is a good time to think about the importance of family links. I have wonderful memories of growing up within an extended family, and know from personal experience just how secure and confident it can make one feel in future life to have been cared for and loved so much, not only by one's parents, but by other relatives. Even if you have different parenting ideas from your own parents or those of your brothers or sisters, try not to let that stand in the way of them sharing the joy of watching your baby grow up. While consistency and routine play a very important part in helping rear confident, happy children, it is also good for your baby to learn how to cope when things are a little different sometimes. So if you leave him overnight with his grandparents, and he stays up too late, or gets his first taste of chocolate, try to be relaxed, and enjoy the pleasure of this grandparent and grandchild bond. Make the most of your time off, enjoy yourself, and you will return to your baby energised and relaxed.

Feeding

- Your baby will still need two to three milk feeds a day, and by one year it is recommended that all drinks are given from a beaker.

- If you have not already done so I would advise you to introduce a beaker first thing in the morning and also mid-afternoon, if he is still having a feed then.

- The bedtime bottle should be replaced with a drink of milk from a beaker by the time he is one year. You can help prepare your baby for this by reducing the amount of milk that you give him in his bottle.

- If he is taking a full 240ml (8oz) feed when he goes to bed, gradually reduce this by 15ml ($^1/_2$oz) every three to four nights until he is taking around 180ml (6oz) .

- Once babies are taking their last milk feed from a beaker, they do tend to cut down on the amount they drink. By doing this gradually over two weeks, he is unlikely to be aware that he is getting less milk.

- Babies who have cut several teeth should be capable of chewing chicken and meat, and this can be served either sliced or diced. If your baby doesn't yet have teeth he will probably still need to have his food pulsed.

Playing with food

The older your baby gets, the more he asserts himself and at mealtimes you may need to be firm if he starts to play up. It is all right to knock over a cup of milk accidentally but it is not all right to turn it upside down deliberately and let all the liquid pour out. Throwing food or swiping it all on to the floor usually means he has had enough. Remove his plate of food and get him down from the table. Tell him that he may eat his food, or he may finish his meal, but he may not throw it. Spilt drinks can be handled with an, 'Oh dear, let's mop it up' whereas deliberately upturning cups means they are removed with a simple but firm, 'Milk is for drinking, not for playing with'.

Sleeping

- Babies of 11 months of age need approximately two and a half to three hours of sleep between the hours of 7am and 7pm, or 8am and 8pm.

- Some babies will start to cut back on the daily amount of sleep they need and I would advise that you keep a close eye on how well your baby is sleeping at night during this stage. Try cutting back the morning nap to 15–20 minutes as it's important to keep the longer nap after lunch so that he doesn't get overtired at bedtime.

- If despite cutting back the morning nap you notice that your baby is not settling so well in the evening, or waking up early, you may need to cut out the morning nap altogether.

The bed and bathtime routine

By now your baby will probably have outgrown his bath seat and he will attempt to move around the bath a lot. It is important that you continue to supervise him at all times when he is in the bath. This is also a good age to begin getting him used to the shower. You can start by taking him in with you and holding him close while you allow a gentle spray of water on his body. As he gets more confident about being in the shower, you can then stand him up, and make a game of washing each other's body. He will enjoy a bedtime story and this might be a good opportunity for Dad to spend some time with him.

Development

Mental development

Your baby can now understand a great deal even if he is only saying one or two distinct words. He will be able to nod 'Yes' and 'No' to simple questions. If you use expressive movements when talking to him he will pick these up quickly and try to copy you.

> **RECOGNITION**
> To encourage your baby's recognition of certain tasks and activites, keep talking to him about what you are doing and also what is going to happen next. Use the same phrases for certain actions such as teeth brushing and getting ready to have a bath.

- He likes to gain your approval but he also has a definite idea of what he wants to do. He may begin to resist his daytime nap and may arch his back and become inflexible if he does not want to sit in his pushchair. He may also attempt to wriggle free from a cuddle when he has seen something he wishes to play with. You will need to distract him to prevent too many flare-ups but some are unavoidable at this age.

- He is becoming better at problem solving and will enjoy the sensation of working things out on his own.

- You may notice that he will anticipate certain things now. He will see you get his coat out and so hold up his arms.

Physical development

As your baby becomes more competent at standing and cruising he may begin to have a few falls and knocks. Try not to over-react to these. Normally a baby cries through the shock of the fall rather than any real pain, unless he has knocked himself against a piece of furniture. Be sympathetic but don't over-react to every tumble. If you are upbeat and calm about it, he will get over it much more quickly. Comfort him if he needs it, then distract him with something new to take his mind off the shock he has had.

> **TOP TIP**
> The phrase 'Oops-a-daisy' or 'All fall down' can be used when he falls to encourage him to get up again without too much fuss.

Encouraging your baby to pass you objects is a good way of teaching her about sharing

Encouraging development through play

Now is a good time to teach him about tidying up his toys. He may not yet be much help and you may think it is easier to do it all yourself, but with some encouragement, he can give you a car or brick or be shown where to put it.

• If you keep his toys sorted into separate boxes, possibly of different colours, he will learn much more quickly where things belong. Keeping his toys in order will help him play with most of them, as you can rotate what comes out each day. It will also help him concentrate on one or two things at a time. If all the construction bricks are kept together, he is far more likely to start to match them up than if they are all mixed up among other toys.

• He will enjoy the company of other babies, but will probably make a grab for them if they are playing with a toy he wants. Use plenty of distraction and keep play sessions with other babies quite short. Make sure there are plenty of similar toys even if it means taking a few of your own as this will help to reduce the inevitable grabs and snatches that may occur.

Toys, games and books

- Add a few new toys to the ones he already has, such as very simple tray puzzles which have knobs for him to hold the pieces. A hammer bench will encourage his hand-eye coordination and he will love to make a loud noise with it.

- Find a few musical toys that he is able to handle. A small tambourine to shake, some shakers and bells will all add to your singing sessions. Put on a CD and encourage him to play along as you sing. Use songs that have a good beat to play a drum with him and encourage his own sense of rhythm. He will love to be danced around the room with you. Singing and dancing can be great ways to jolly him out of moods if he seems to get frustrated quickly by his toys or explorations.

- Helping him drum or hammer refines his hand skills. He may now be able to turn the pages of his board books and will delight in doing so. Keep his attention by asking him to point to pictures of things he recognises. Draw his attention to the cat in the picture with additional information, e.g. 'Grandma has a cat; hers is black'. This will help him make the connection that the cats in pictures and reality may not all look quite the same but they are all still cats.

Musical toys help develop her hand-eye co-ordination

- Point out primary colours to him in his books, e.g. 'The cup is red, your boots are red', so he learns to make connections and see similarities in things. There are some excellent books on the market that deal with colours and opposites. Although he won't fully understand these concepts yet, giving him plenty of examples will help his growing awareness and understanding.

- Play lots of 'give-and-take' games with him so that he learns the basis of sharing. He will not be ready to share toys with other babies for a while but getting the idea across now will help. If you ask him to give you a piece of his toast, thank him when he does and offer him a piece of yours.

Books about colour will help her learn to make connections and see similarities in the world around her

Q&A

shy baby

Q

How can I get my eleven-month-old daughter Kate to be less wary of people? We live in a small village, which is a close and friendly community. Until about a month ago, Kate would smile happily at everyone, but now she turns her head away when people speak to her. My neighbour, who Kate has known since birth, would love to look after her occasionally, but Kate just wants to be beside me the whole time. I tried leaving Kate last week for an hour, but it was a disaster and in the end I brought her home as she was crying so much.

A

This is all part of Kate's emotional development as she is beginning to be aware of new situations and unfamiliar people. A few months ago she would respond to any smiling face, but now she is more discerning. This wariness of strangers is connected with a growing anxiety about being separated from you and this phase often coincides with the time a baby learns to crawl. She now has the means to leave you, and has realised that you can also leave her.

Coping with this milestone needs gentle handling. It will usually peak between 10 and 18 months. These months can feel overwhelming as she clings to your side, but it is a phase and it will pass. Be aware and sympathetic, but also help her to overcome some of her anxiety.

When out in the village, greet people yourself, talk to Kate about who you are meeting and let Kate respond with a smile if she wishes. Explain to others that Kate is feeling a bit shy today. Some adults have forgotten or don't understand this period in a baby's life and may try to get too close to her. Put yourself in her position. Being approached by an unfamiliar person who wants to touch you straight away is a most disconcerting feeling.

Some babies become very clingy even in their own homes. They cannot bear it if you so much as leave the room. Overwhelming as it is, try to keep Kate in view, scooping her up as you move around the house, rather than trying to slip upstairs quickly. Playing games of 'Peekaboo' or 'Hide-and-seek' will help her to understand that, even if she can't see something, it is still there.

If you haven't already joined a mother and toddler group, try to find one locally. This will help both you and her to socialise in a safe setting. She may sit near you for the first few sessions, but once her confidence grows she will begin to crawl away fascinated by the other children. Also, getting her used to staying for short periods with someone other than immediate family is a good idea. Have a regular cup of coffee with your neighbour and let Kate become familiar with the surroundings. Once you feel she is used to the house, try leaving her there for a short time. Take one or two favourite toys and go inside the house to settle her in. Give her ten minutes' warning that you are leaving, but will be back soon. Don't sneak out, even if she appears content. That will only make her more anxious about you leaving her. She may cry as you leave, but keep smiling and tell her you will see her later. Make the first separation a short one. Twenty minutes to half an hour is long enough. Build up the time very slowly, unless she appears quite happy with the arrangement. This period in a baby's life can be difficult for you as it may feel as if you have no life of your own. Don't worry – this is all part of motherhood. And spending a short time on your own will benefit everyone.

The Twelfth Month

Y OUR BABY HAS REACHED THE AGE OF ONE YEAR. HE IS FAST BECOMING a toddler, and you will soon be presented with plenty of exciting new challenges and experiences. This is a good month to reflect on the many magical milestones of your baby's life so far. Flicking back through the pages of this book I am sure you will find it hard to believe how many incredible 'firsts' your baby has achieved. First smile, first tooth, first time he grasped a toy, first time he rolled over. The list is endless and amazing. But, as you reflect on all the changes in your baby's short life, it is important that you take some time to reflect on the changes in your life, too.

The things you used to consider part of your everyday life – trips to the hair-dresser, gym or cinema; giggly, gossipy lunches with girlfriends – may now come very low on your list of priorities. Start thinking about how you might be able to fit some of these activities back into your life again. Being a good mother is not about being a martyr. A happy home life – and that includes a happy fulfilled mother – is the most important gift you can give your child. To protect this, take the time to focus on your own needs, and those of your husband.

Time goes so quickly when you are a parent, and there will be many more magical milestones in the years ahead. So every now and then it is important to remember that you were a 'girl' before you were a mother. Try to fit some baby-free time in, meet up every now and again with friends where the talk is not all about babies. Treat yourself to a new hair-do, a glamorous pair of shoes, or whatever it takes to remind yourself of the 'girl' in you. Do not feel guilty about spoiling yourself now and again – you deserve it!

Feeding

- By the age of 12 months babies still need between 350ml (12oz) and 500ml (18oz) a day of milk.

- This is usually divided into two or three drinks and is inclusive of milk used in cooking or on cereals.

- To determine the right amount of milk for your baby you should look at how well he is eating his solids. If he is getting very fussy over his food, then keep him to the minimum amount. This should be divided between two to three feeds.

- He should be taking all of his milk from a beaker by the time he reaches his first birthday.

COW'S MILK
Full-fat pasteurised cow's milk can be given to drink at the age of one year. If your baby refuses cow's milk, try gradually diluting his formula with it until he is happy to take full cow's milk. If possible, try to give your baby organic milk as it is higher in Omega 3 fatty acids than most non-organic milk. Omega 3 fatty acids are essential for maintaining a healthy heart, supple and flexible joints, healthy growth and strong bones and teeth.

A variety of flavours

This is a good age to start widening the variety of foods your baby is having. Introducing recipes from other countries and reducing the spices will encourage him to accept stronger flavours. It will make things easier when you are abroad if he is used to eating foods other than traditional English ones.

You should be encouraging your baby to eat much of his meal by himself using a spoon and you may notice he will use his spoon to stir as well as dig into food. When he reaches one year you can also introduce a baby fork. He may find it easier than a spoon, especially if you show him how to dig it into cubes of food such as meat. Use a bowl that has divisions so that he can see all the individual ingredients in each division and can decide what he wants to eat.

EATING WITH THE FAMILY
Now your baby is able to self-feed effectively and is enjoying a wide range of foods he can join in with most of the meals you make for the rest of the family. But remember not to add any sugar or salt to his foods. If necessary, take out his portion of food before adding seasoning for the rest of the family.

Sleeping

- Babies of 12 months of age need approximately two to three hours sleep between the hours of 7am and 7pm, or 8am and 8pm.

- You may find that your baby starts to cut out his morning nap, or will only take a catnap of 10 minutes when out and about in the car or buggy. When this happens you can, if need be, allow him a longer nap at lunchtime, so that he does not get too exhausted for any activities that you have planned for the afternoon.

Development

Mental development

- Your child is making the transition from baby to toddler and will be demonstrating his independence in many ways. His language will be developing fast. Although he probably only has a few words, he can understand a great deal. Despite his increasing desire to be independent, he will still like to be with you and will want to play with you a lot.

- His memory is developing and he will recognise places and remember where toys are, even when they are out of sight. He will be able to anticipate activities, and will assist in getting dressed by raising his foot or putting his arms up.

- You may have heard your baby's first word by his first birthday, or he may already have two or three. The first word is often 'Dada' or 'Bye, bye'. He may also be able to name items such as his cup, a book or a dog. You will know what the words are, even if they are not really clear, as he will use them in the right situations. You may notice that he dribbles less now, which shows that he is gaining control over his tongue, lips and mouth ready for speech.

- He will be able to follow a simple instruction which may contain an action

such as, 'Wave bye, bye'. He will know all the names of his immediate family and may try to say them when asked.

• Occasionally, a one-year-old child will show considerable perception by demonstrating empathy and an ability to copy adult behaviour. Children as young as one, sometimes 'mother' a toy by giving the dolly a drink or pretending to feed it. Signs such as these are often most evident in pre-school children while they are playing independently, so you could try and watch your baby at play without him realising you are doing so.

• Your baby will now begin to copy all he sees. He will want to be near you and will enjoy 'helping'. Even at this age he may try to imitate you by trying to wipe the floor or a tabletop with a cloth. To him, everything that happens in his day is interesting, so encourage him to join in your chores.

- Your baby will be very affectionate towards you, giving kisses if he feels like it and when asked. He will also show that he has a temper, especially when he cannot do what he wants. Deal with these outbursts calmly. If he seems to have a lot of them, take a look at his day and see if he needs more time outside, more time playing physically or perhaps just his toys rotated so that he has some less familiar ones to play with.

- By now your baby may begin to enjoy the company of other babies. He may show a preference for his own gender and may play alongside another baby of a similar age. If there are older children present he will actively engage with them as he finds them fascinating. He may still be wary of strangers and may not like to be left; although once you have gone he should be quite content if he is in familiar surroundings.

Physical development

By the time your baby celebrates his first birthday he will be well on the way to leaving babyhood behind. He may have taken his first step, although many babies do not walk independently until 14–15 months. By one year, most babies are capable of pulling themselves up, using cot bars or furniture.

- If your baby is not yet walking he will enjoy being 'walked' by you. He may also like to push a baby walker truck or other wheeled toy as this gives him a sense of the freedom he will have when walking independently.

- His physical development will enable him to sit down from a standing position more easily, by bending at the knees and sliding himself down. It is a skill worth teaching him as often a baby will pull up to a standing.

Your child is making the transition from baby to toddler and will be demonstrating his independence in many ways

position in his cot and will then be unable to get back down again. Each time you put him in his cot, let him hold on to the rails and cover his hands, teaching him how to slide them down as he lowers himself.

- Your baby's sight is fully developed and he is now able to see as well as an adult.

- He may be showing a preference for using one hand rather than the other when playing or eating.

Encouraging development through play

Although you may encourage him by holding out your hands and seeing if he will walk to you, he will take his first steps when he is ready and feels confident enough to do it.

Your baby will start to walk when he is ready: you can encourage his walking, however, by supporting him as he makes attempts to do so

- He will be able to build brick towers more proficiently now, perhaps using three or more bricks. He will be better at tray puzzles and sorting shapes as his dexterity has improved. He may be a little apprehensive of new puzzles until he realises that they need the same actions as those he is familiar with.

- In the bath and in water play you may notice he can now pour using either hand. If he has a tea set he may set things out in order, putting the spoon into the cup and then setting the cup on a saucer.

- If you find some chunky wax crayons and a piece of paper your baby may manage to make marks on it. It will not be long before he realises that the pens you use make marks too, so remember to keep felt tips and biros well out of reach from now on.

- Your baby will now be able to throw quite well. Discourage any throwing in the house, even with soft balls. Try to keep them for rolling only. Take him out into the garden or park where he can throw as much as he likes.

- When he is playing alone you may notice him beginning to use fantasy play with his toys. He may offer his teddies a drink or pretend to stir with a spoon and cup.

- Talk to your baby as much as you can about all you are doing. Begin to teach him his body parts. He will quickly be able to point to or touch many parts such as nose, ears, mouth, tummy and so on.

- Continue to make times in the day when you encourage your baby to play for short periods alone. You can sit near by but be occupied doing something else. Because a baby of this age can be quite vocal and demanding in his need for attention it is easy to let these times of solitary play slip, especially as he is now good company as well. It is good for him to have to amuse himself for a while so that he is not solely reliant on you for his amusement.

Toys, games and books

If relatives ask you what your baby would like for his first birthday, suggest plenty of tray puzzles, more complex shape sorters and bath toys including ones which squirt, pour and float. There are many available and as they will be used on a daily basis for some time they will prove good value for money.

- Your baby may like simple glove or finger puppets although you will probably have to place them on his hand for him to begin with.

- He is ready now for simple art activities such as chunky crayons and non-toxic paint.

- Simple playdough sets with a rolling pin and cutters are also suitable. These kinds of activities will need your supervision but

THE STAIRS
Even if not walking your baby will be more confident about tackling stairs. If you stand behind him he may manage to climb a whole flight, using his hands and knees. Continue to teach him how to come down safely backwards. Once he has learnt this technique he may come down quite quickly sliding on his tummy.

It is good for your baby to play for short periods alone as this will encourage her independence

they will give him hours of pleasure and plenty of learning opportunities.

• As he learns to walk your baby may enjoy a simple sit-and-ride toy. These need his feet to propel them, and are ideal for this age. If he does not have a baby truck already, then buy him a sturdy one to encourage his walking and also give him something to carry or push his favourite toys in.

• One item he will enjoy for a year or more is his own chair. This could be bought with a small table. Check for sturdiness, as some can tip over easily. He will enjoy sitting here to do puzzles or look at books and it will mark the beginning of his toddler years.

TOP TIP
Begin to store paper, as in the months to come you will use a lot of it as your baby starts drawing and painting.

Sturdy sit-and-ride toys will encourage your baby's walking as he uses his feet to move them along

Q&A

staying with friends

Q

We are going to stay with my aunt and uncle in a couple of months, when our daughter, Jessie, will be a year old.

I am very apprehensive about how we will manage with a crawler in their house. It is quite large and is full of antiques and the stairs are steep and twisty. It is not really a child-friendly environment.

Can you give me any advice regarding what I could take with me to 'child-proof' the house a little and to help Jessie settle in strange surroundings?

A

Depending on how well you know your relatives, you may be able to talk to them beforehand about taking Jessie and what her needs will be at the time. If they have never had children and are unaware of the dangers in the home, they may be grateful if you make a few tactful suggestions as to how you will manage. If you are concerned about dangers from the stairs, consider taking a foldaway travel barrier. This could be used across the doorway of the room where Jessie will sleep.

Many old houses do not have standard width stairs, so the gate could always be moved downstairs by day and used to prevent Jessie leaving the area you will be in and getting on to the stairs.

Make yourself up a small pack of the most useful 'child-proofing' products. Include at least four socket covers, a set of corner protectors, two door slam stoppers, and a few short bungees (use these to keep cupboard doors shut) or cabinet slide locks. These should be enough to make the area that Jessie will be in as safe as possible, although she will still need to be watched. Pack a small first aid kit with plasters, antiseptic cream, Arnica cream (for bruises), baby paracetamol, teething gel and a thermometer. This should cover most medical emergencies.

If you are not travelling too far, why not take an insulated bag with some frozen meals for Jessie? This would cut down on your meal preparation time in a strange kitchen and also give her some familiarity. As well as Jessie's cot and bedding, take one or two familiar toys from her cot and favourite books with you. Going to bed in a strange house can be daunting at this age. Pack a plug-in night-light, even if she sleeps in darkness, as it is useful to have it

plugged in to check on her or deal with her in the night. Pack your baby monitor, as you may not be able to hear her in a large house. If you have a small CD player, why not take that along, together with some soothing music or her familiar nursery rhymes. This can all help her settle in.

When you first arrive at the house, try to look for any potential dangers and find the best place to set up Jessie's play area. Don't feel embarrassed about asking if some things such as trailing wires or table lamps can be moved if they are in her 'area'. It will be much easier than apologising for a lamp that has been pulled over and broken. Look for hanging window cords, unstable furniture, sharp corners, houseplants, heaters and ornaments at reachable levels.

Decide on a rota with your husband so one of you is always 'in charge' of Jessie. This leaves the other parent able to relax a little more or have a lie-in.

Taking a baby away to an unfamiliar place does take thought, but can also be an enriching experience for you all.

rough play with Dad

Q

What are the dangers of rough play with a twelve-month-old? My husband likes to play with James in a very physical way, which leaves me unable to watch. However, James seems to love it and will cling to his father's legs begging for more. Is rough play just a father/son thing?

A

There are some dangers in rough play with babies, but if both baby and father enjoy such times then, given a few guidelines, there is no reason to stop your husband. In fact, babies and small children benefit from this kind of play. It is mostly instigated by men and is part of their bonding process with their child. It helps a child learn self-control and self-confidence, and gives them an awareness of their bodies. Fathers may be unable to explain why they play like this with their children, but it seems to be an instinctive way of communicating.

All babies love and crave movement. They have a highly developed vestibular system, which originates in the inner ear and is responsible for their sense of balance and perception of movement. Small babies love rocking, swaying or being pushed in the pram, as it soothes this system and helps them to relax.

At between six and 12 months, a baby gains more control over his head muscles. His vestibular system is now at its most sensitive and he enjoys movement of all kinds, especially rocking and bouncing. Head banging can also become an issue at this time. But with the growing awareness of 'shaken baby syndrome', it is important to know what is and isn't safe. No father would want their baby to be hurt with this type of play, so explaining the dangers and giving some guidelines is sensible:

Don't let your baby's head flop around, and be aware of your baby's ability to control it. This means that actually throwing a baby in the air should be avoided, but by all means 'fly' them while securely holding their body with both hands.

Don't swing your baby by the arms or hands, as his joints are still loose and are easily dislocated.

If James is crawling, encourage your husband to 'chase' him. Provide them with a tunnel of some kind and they will both enjoy it.

A session of tickling can produce squeals of laughter, but be aware that some babies have a lower tolerance level than others. The laughter you hear is involuntary. It is the body's response to the stimulation of pain receptors in the skin. Watch your baby's face or body language for signs that he has had enough.

Useful addresses

Baby equipment
The Great Little Trading Company
Pondwood Close
Moulton Park
Noarthampton NN3 6DF
Tel: 0870 850 6000
www.gltc.co.uk

Breast pumps
Ameda Egnell Ltd
Unit 2, Belvedere Trading Estate
Taunton
Somerset TA1 1BH
Tel: 01823 336362

Maternity bras
www.expressyourselfbras.co.uk

Organisations
Foundation for the Study of Infant Deaths
Artillery House
11-19 Artillery Row
London SW1P 1RT
Helpline: 020 7233 2090
www.sids.org.uk

La Leche League
PO Box 29
West Bridgeford
Nottingham
NG2 7NPA
Tel: 020 7242 1278
Helpline: 0845 120 2918
www.laleche.org.uk

The National Childbirth Trust
Alexandra House

Oldham Terrace
London W3 6NH
Tel:0870 444 8707 (general enquiries)
Tel:0870 444 8708 (breastfeeding helpline)
www.nctpregnancyandbabycare.com

St John Ambulance
27 St John's Lane
London EC1M 4BU
Tel: 020 7324 4000
www.sja.org.uk

Twins and Multiple Births Association (TAMBA)
2 The Willows
Gardner Road
Guildford
GU1 4PG
Tel: 0870 770 3305
Twinline: 0870 138 0509
www.tamba.org.uk

Further reading

Byam-Cook, Clare, *What to Expect When You're Breastfeeding... And What If You Can't?*, Vermilion, 2006

Ford, Gina, and Beer, Alice, *A Contented House with Twins*, Vermilion, 2006

Ford, Gina, *The New Contented Little Baby Book*, Vermilion, 2006

Ford, Gina, *The Contented Little Baby Book of Weaning*, Vermilion 2006

Woolfson, Dr Richard, *What is My Baby Thinking*, Hamlyn, 2006

Index

A

affection 158, 196, 225
age gap 198–9
allergies 140, 141
animals 179, 195
anticipation 90, 106, 110, 215, 223
art activities 228, 229, 230

B

baby bouncer 148
baby wipes 21
balls 162, 228
barrier cream 21, 23, 24, 126, 157
baths 16, 50–52, 64, 104, 180
  bath seat 144
  safety 51, 104
  toys 72, 94, 130, 144, 228
beaker 155, 171, 187, 200, 212, 222
  learning to use 141
bedtime 47–8, 151, 157
bibs 142
birthmarks 11
biting 127
blankets 54, 71, 156, 167
bonding 16, 60, 196, 233
books 78, 79, 95, 111, 130, 149, 162, 189, 190–91, 208
boredom 19, 26, 120, 152
bottle-feeding 37–42
  equipment 39
  expressed milk 37
  getting enough 65, 70
  giving feed 41–2
  making-up feeds 40–41
  overfeeding 39–40

positioning 41
weaning onto bottle 102, 120
wind 26, 42
bottles 39
  cleaning/sterilising 41, 43
bottom shuffling 175, 191
bowel movements 23
breakfast 132, 135, 139, 155, 171
breastfeeding 14–15, 32
  counsellor 14, 34, 37, 70
  dropping feeds 102
  establishing 32
  fore and hind milk 15, 32–3
  getting enough 36, 65, 69–70
  leakages 32
  let-down reflex 32, 36
  milk coming in 14, 15
  milk supply 25, 70
  positioning 14, 34, 35–6, 70
  and return to work 102, 120
  weaning onto bottle 102, 120
  see also expressing
breast pads 32
breast pump 37, 120
breathing 12, 59
bug socks 111
buggy 47, 72, 91, 182
burping 16, 19, 42–3

C

Caesarean section 34
calm 32, 37, 48, 50, 56, 116
candida rash 24
carers 101, 116–17, 166–7
chairs, baby 61, 68, 125, 230
changing, see nappies, changing

changing mat 21, 22
check-up, eight-month 176–8
childcare 101, 114, 116–18, 166–7
childminders 116, 167
children 94, 98, 179, 189, 198, 204, 26–17, 225
clingy baby 144, 174, 209, 219
colds 168, 170–71
colic 15, 26–8, 33
colostrum 13
comforters 90, 124, 151, 162
communication 56, 57, 63
concentration 105, 129, 158, 144
conversations 63, 74, 82, 108–9, 161, 202
cooking 164
co-ordination 91, 98, 107, 158
copying 63, 144, 146, 172, 204, 215, 224–5
cord stump 12, 64
cot 53, 71
cot bumpers 53
cot death 53, 60, 71
cradle cap 64
crawling 60, 146–7, 159, 162, 168, 175, 190, 205
cruising 176, 190, 205
crying: controlled 28
crying down 24–5, 26
  newborn 24–9, 58
  reasons for 25–9, 58
cupboard locks 163, 191
curiosity 77, 206

D

demand-feeding 28
diary 48, 86, 140, 200
diet, mother's 28, 32, 70, 121
discipline 126, 213

dressing 16, 63, 204, 223
drinks 32, 70, 141, 155, 164, 199, 200
drooling 126, 157, 223
dummies 40, 90

E

early-morning waking 121, 200
emotional responses 124, 162
engorgement 14, 15, 102
exercise 78, 84, 93, 150, 152
expressing 14, 24, 28, 36–7, 154
    for growth spurts 70, 87
    storing milk 37
    technique 37
    at work 120–21
eye contact 60, 63, 74
eyes 11, 50–51, 58
    see also vision

F

faces, recognising 61, 74, 84
facial expressions 114
family 66, 198–9, 204, 212, 222
fathers 122, 179, 196, 214, 233
feeding: on demand 28
    distractions 105
    dropping feeds 119
    'feeding all night'
        syndrome 15
    first feed 13–14
    handling baby 16
    at night 28, 29, 39, 64–5,
        69, 86, 120, 135–6, 154, 170
    overfeeding 26, 39–40
    preparing for 35–6
    routine 14, 15, 38, 69–70
    split feeds 65, 86
    time between feeds 26
    see also bottle-feeding;
        breast-feeding; solid foods
finger foods 155–6, 157, 171, 181, 187
fingers 10, 76, 81, 90–91, 93
fire risks 164
fist aid kit 232
fontanelles 11
food, see solid foods
forceps delivery 11
formula 38, 39, 40–42

fretful baby 18, 19
fruit juice 141, 155, 187, 200
frustration 127, 130, 158, 209

C

gag reflex 59
games 79, 81, 93, 98, 109, 110, 130, 144, 148, 161, 162, 180, 218
GP 24, 40, 42, 59, 64, 69, 158, 170, 176, 205
grandparents 116, 166, 175, 212
grasp 76, 80, 93, 98, 108, 125, 146
    pincer 146, 156, 161, 176, 205
    reflex 10, 60, 74, 81
groups and classes 150
    exercise 78, 84, 150, 152
    mother and baby 66, 84, 94, 219
growth spurts 24, 36, 70, 87, 101

H

hair 11, 51, 64
    pulling 122
    washing 143, 144
hand-eye co-ordination 91, 98, 107, 217
handling baby 16–19, 77
hands 60, 76, 81, 93, 146, 178
handregard 93
    preference 205, 226
head 11
    control 16, 59, 60, 79, 125, 233
    lifting 59, 60–61, 76, 91, 107
    turning 91
health visitor 13, 40, 42, 59, 69, 205
hearing 56, 74, 81–2, 105
    tests 78, 177
hiccups 59
highchair 140
holding baby 17, 18–19, 51, 71
holidays 182, 142
humour, sense of 182, 189
hunger 25, 36, 38, 39, 49, 58, 102
hygiene 37, 39, 41, 136

I

immunisation 73, 88, 105
infections 170
interaction 60, 74, 159
iron 134, 135, 140

K

kicking 61, 68, 77, 91, 129

L

language 223
latching on 13, 14, 34, 35–6
laughing 91, 106, 111
learning 162
leaving baby 68–9, 101, 219
let-down reflex 32, 36
libraries 149
lighting, subdued 50, 58, 72
loneliness 58, 66
lunch 132, 135, 138

M

massage 50, 52–3, 60, 78, 112
mastitis 102
matching 208
me time 69, 101, 152, 196, 220
meals 132, 152, 171–2, 181, 222
meconium 23
memory 109, 110, 111, 223
milk: cow's 222
milky foods 187, 199
    reducing intake 134, 139, 213
        requirements 65
        see also breast milk; for-
            mula
mirrors 94, 105
mobiles 63, 77, 78
moro reflex 49, 59–60, 74, 87
Moses basket 53
mouthing 90, 108, 202
music 81–2, 90, 95, 150, 217

N

nails, trimming 10
name, recognising 148, 202
nannies 116
nappies 21–4

changing 16, 20–24, 64
leaving off 20, 24, 77
liners 21, 22
nappy rash 20, 24
navel 64
neck control 16, 17, 59, 60, 77, 91, 107
newborn baby 10–29, 126
night feeds 28, 29, 39, 55, 64–5, 69, 86, 135–6, 154, 170
night waking 157, 171
nipples, sore 14, 34, 36
'no', saying 126, 158, 175, 179
noise 56, 90, 96, 204
nursery 118, 151, 198
nursery rhymes 78, 191–2, 206–7
nursing chair 34, 41
nursing pillow 34–5

O

oils 24, 52, 53, 64
outings 66, 72, 84, 114, 152, 180, 196, 207, 210
overheating 44, 53, 54, 71, 83
overstimulation 16, 25, 60, 61
overtiredness 16, 18, 25–6, 87, 157, 200

P

paracetamol, baby 73
patting 26, 49, 122, 158
personality 84, 112, 184–5
pets 195
photo album 130,174–5
picking up baby 16, 17
pillows and cushions 34, 35, 41
plants 165
play: fantasy 228
physical 179, 225, 233
playing alone 77, 78, 109, 113, 159, 209, 28
playgroups 95
play gym 61, 68, 77, 78, 81, 91
play mat 109
playpen 129, 147
possetting 42
premature baby 11, 43, 56, 64
protein 140–1
push-ups 77, 94, 107, 131

putting baby down 16, 17

R

rattles 63, 78, 81, 94–5, 110–11
reaching 93, 125
reading 79, 95, 108, 189
reflexes 59–60
reflux 42
rest 32, 70, 121
rocking 26, 49, 71
rocking chairs 34
rolling 22, 93, 107, 109, 124, 147, 167, 178
room temperature 50, 52, 55, 71
rooting reflex 59
routine 28, 96–7, 166–7
7 am to 7 pm routine 46–7, 64
establishing 14, 15, 68–9
feeding 68–9
sleep 46–7, 55
starting nursery 151

S

safety 22, 107, 125, 159, 163–5, 179, 191, 232
bath 51, 104, 174
sleep 53–5
sand play 194
scratch mittens 10
separation anxiety 124, 130, 144, 161, 204, 209, 219
settling baby 16, 48–9, 56
self-settling 25, 49, 71, 174
shampoo 64
showering 214
shyness 219
siblings 198–9
singing 56, 81, 90, 111, 130, 146, 161, 217
sitting 107, 114, 124, 131, 147, 148, 175
in cot 174
from standing 225–6
skin 12, 20, 21
sleep: associations 26, 28, 47, 49, 71, 83, 167
in big cot 71
naps out of cot 47, 72, 96,

121,   143, 223
poor sleepers 55
position 53, 54, 60, 71, 103, 156, 167
rhythms 46, 49, 71–2
routine 46–7, 55
safety 53–5
through the night 55
sleeping bag 54, 87, 104, 156, 167
smell, sense of 56
smiling 74, 78, 84, 91, 105, 124
soft play areas 210
solid foods 155, 171–2, 199
appearance 172, 181
consistency 136, 171, 187, 199, 213
finger foods 155–6, 171, 181, 187
first-stage foods 136, 138–9
first meal 137–8
freezing 139
messy eating 187, 141–2
playing with 172, 187, 213
preparing 136–7
refusing 181, 199–200
second-stage foods 140–41
self-feeding 140, 146, 156, 172, 181, 187, 199, 222
spicy 222
see also weaning
speech development 192
conversations 63, 74, 82, 108–9, 161, 202
sounds 63, 74, 84, 89, 98, 144–5, 161, 175, 177, 202
words 168, 175, 188–9, 202, 207, 215, 223
stairs 205, 229, 232
gates 163, 205
standing 77, 129, 148, 161, 168, 176, 190
in cot 200–201
staying with friends 96–7, 232
sterilising 37, 39, 41, 136
strangers 105, 122, 124, 174, 219, 225
suckling reflex 59
sucky baby 39–40
sugar water 28, 29
swaddling 44–5, 49, 71
half-swaddling 71, 83, 87

swimming 84, 95, 108, 152

T

talking to baby 17, 51–2, 56, 60, 112, 158, 192, 228
taste 58, 77
teatime 135, 139, 172, 181
teats 39
teeth cleaning 127, 157
teething 126–7, 131, 157, 158
temper 225
testes 178
thumb-sucking 107
tiredness 25, 58, 196
toes 10, 60, 125, 129
toys 26, 98, 175–6, 204, 206, 209
    favourite 162

household items 127–9, 192, 206–7
    musical 217
    push-along 193, 225, 230
    sit-and-ride 230
    storing 216
    tidying away 216
tickling 161, 233
treasure basket 207–8
tummy time 60–61, 79, 94, 95, 108
twins 185

V

vernix 12
vision 26, 58, 61, 74, 161, 176, 177, 226
visitors, limiting 15–16

voice: recognising 56, 61, 74, 105

W

walking 190, 225, 226
    reflex 59
water, boiled 40, 141, 155, 187
water play 94, 130, 193–4, 228
waving 125
weaning 132, 134–42
    early 102, 119–20, 135
    signs of readiness 135–6
    see also solid foods
weight gain 26, 28, 39–40, 69
wind 19, 26, 35, 42
    see also burping
work, return to 102, 114, 157, 166, 173

About the author

For many years Gina Ford was regarded as one of the most sought-after maternity nurses in the world, specialising in caring for babies and toddlers with serious sleeping and feeding problems. She worked in many parts of the world with hundreds of different families and was nominated by *Harpers & Queen* as one of the top ten maternity nurses in the country.

Gina's first book, *The Contented Little Baby Book*, was published in 1999. It was a runaway success, largely due to enthusiastic personal recommendation, its matter-of-fact style and practical approach. Now fully revised and updated, it has consistently been one of the UK's bestselling parenting books. In 2004 Gina recognised that despite the wealth of parenting information available, many mothers still felt isolated. In an effort to fill the gap, Gina launched www.contentedbaby.com and, in the process, created a wonderful, supportive and dynamic on-line community. It is an amazing forum where parents from all over the world share their experiences and help support each other on all aspects of following the Contented Little Baby philosophy.

Gina has gone on to write a further nine highly successful childcare books, and, as a great advocate of reading with babies and toddlers, she has also created the Tom and Ella series of beautifully illustrated board books for babies and toddlers. Gina is also launching The Contented Baby Trust, a charitable organisation, aimed at supporting mothers who are following the Contented Baby methods. For more details go to www.contentedbabypressoffice.com

Acknowledgements

I would like to thank the following for all their help on this book: the team at Vermilion – Fiona MacIntyre, Imogen Fortes, Nicky Henderson, Nicky Stonehill and Katherine Hockley; my agent Emma Kirby; advisors Dr Richard Woolfson, Russell Nathan, Paul Hosford, Rory Jenkins, Frances Howard Brown, Clare Byam-Cook and Dr Philippa Rundle; my family and friends – W A Ford, Andrew and Jean Fair, Ann Clough, Sheila Eskdale, Jane Revell, Carla Fodden Flint and Yamini Franzini. A special thank you to all the wonderful parents who continue to send me their messages of support and all the beautiful babies who feature in the book: Grace, Faith, Lily, Owen, George, Sonny, Neve, Jacob, Rose, Emilia, Lila, Oscar, Joe, Julia, Lauren, Anton, Leonard, Isabel, Hazel, Buddy, Hugo, Enzo, Harry, Annaleise, Edie and Storm.